AN INTRODUCTION TO THE HOLY SPIRIT

COMPILED BY HAYES PRESS

Published by:

HAYES PRESS Publisher, Resources & Media,

The Barn, Flaxlands

Royal Wootton Bassett

Swindon, SN4 8DY

United Kingdom

www.hayespress.org

---

1. http://www.Lockman.org

CHAPTER ONE: THE HOLY SPIRIT'S DEITY AND PERSONALITY (REG JONES)

The Bible starts with the word God without giving any explanation of who God is, and in the second verse we are introduced to the Spirit of God. The word for God in Genesis 1:1 is plural, whereas the verb created is singular. This illustrates the truth that there is more than one Person in the Godhead, but they act in unity. The second verse of Genesis 1 refers to one of those Persons in the Godhead as the Spirit of God. Thus very early in the divine record the Deity of God's Holy Spirit is implied.

In Hebrew there are three ways of indicating number by the verb and noun forms; these are singular, dual and plural. Most other languages have only singular and plural. In Genesis 1:7, God is in the plural form and so is the verb "made". From this, some Bible students argue that there are more than two Persons in the Godhead and they worked as One to create the heaven and the earth.

Again in Genesis chapter 1, we see the plurality of the Godhead when God said, "Let Us make man" (v.26). Jewish expositors hold that the use of plurals in reference to God indicates the plural of majesty, so upholding the Unitarian view. This we reject as being inconsistent with other scriptures referred to in this chapter.

There are three Persons in the Godhead as witnessed by statements in Matthew 28:19 and 2 Corinthians 13:14, but as the Jews do not believe in the Trinity they quote Deuteronomy 6:4,

"Hear, O Israel: the LORD our God is one LORD" in support. But the literal rendering here is "Jehovah our Elohim is one Jehovah". Now Elohim is a Hebrew plural and the word one translates a Hebrew word indicating "composite" rather than "unitary". It is more than the Trinity acting as one, it is an inherent oneness within the Godhead - one God.

There is plenty of evidence in the Old Testament for the operation of the Holy Spirit, as witness Psalm 51:11 and Isaiah 63:10. Men prophesied under the direction of the Holy Spirit (Numbers 11:17,26,29) and He enabled men to speak powerful God-given words of encouragement (1 Chronicles 12:18). The Holy Spirit gave David the pattern of the great temple to be erected by his son Solomon. The Spirit of the Lord came upon men of valour to strengthen and encourage them in fighting the Lord's battles; for example, Othniel (Judges 3:10), Gideon (Judges 6:34), Jephthah (Judges 11:29), Samson (Judges 13:25; 14:6,19 etc.).

An important activity of the Holy Spirit in Old Testament times was the inspiration of Scripture, especially noticeable with reference to Messianic prophecies (See 2 Samuel 23:2; 1 Peter 1:10-12).

If the Holy Spirit is God then He must have the attributes of God and the following scriptures testify to this:

(a) The Holy Spirit is eternal (Hebrews 9:14).

(b) The Holy Spirit is omnipresent (Psalm 139:7).

(c) The Holy Spirit is omniscient (1 Corinthians 2:11).

(d) The Holy Spirit is omnipotent (Matthew 12:28).

(e) The Holy Spirit can see everything (1 Corinthians 2:9,10).

(f) The Holy Spirit, in conjunction with the Father and the Son, is the Creator (Job 33:4)

(g) The new birth is brought about by the life-imparting activities of the Holy Spirit (John 1:11-13; 3:5-7; 1 Peter 1:23).

The Holy Spirit is linked with the Father and the Son in the following two scriptures which we have already mentioned: Matthew 28:19 and 2 Corinthians 13:14. Note particularly that in the Matthew scripture the Trinity has only one Name: it is not the Names of the Father, Son and Holy Spirit but the Name of the Father and of the Son and of the Holy Spirit. When Peter was facing Ananias with his deceit he tells him he has lied to the Holy Spirit, whereas in the next verse he says that Ananias has not lied to men but to God (Acts 5:3,4). The Holy Spirit is therefore clearly seen to be God. The comparison of the scripture from Jeremiah 31 and its quotation in the epistle to the Hebrews shows that the Holy Spirit is God. In Jeremiah 31:33 the words of the prophecy are attributed to the Lord whereas when they are quoted for us in Hebrews 10:15 and 16 they are attributed to the Holy Spirit. This truth is further borne out in Matthew 12:31 where speaking against the Holy Spirit is described as blasphemy.

The Holy Spirit is referred to in many different ways in the Bible, showing so conclusively His inherent oneness with both the Father and the Son:

- Acts 16:7: The Spirit of Jesus,
- 2 Corinthians 3:3: Spirit of the Living God,

- 2 Corinthians 3:18: The Lord the Spirit,
- 1 Peter 1:11: The Spirit of Christ.

Having shown that the Holy Spirit is God there is really no need to "prove" that He is a Person, for our God is a personal God - man was made in the image of God and we all have personality. The Holy Spirit likewise has personality. It is interesting to note the various things that are said about Him in Scripture which show Him to be a Person who acts gently and humbly (see for example Nehemiah 9:20; Psalm 143:10; John 1:32; Romans 8:26; Galatians 5:22,23).

CHAPTER TWO: THE HOLY SPIRIT'S INSPIRATION OF SCRIPTURE (ROBERT SHAW)

"How can we know that Scripture is from God without taking refuge in the book itself? It is as if we asked how we can distinguish between light and darkness, white and black, sweet and bitter. Scripture bears in itself no less evidence of its truth than white and black things of their colour or sweet thing of their taste" - Calvin.

"All Scripture is inspired by God" (2 Timothy 3:16 Revised Standard Version). "All Scripture" means the whole of that Scripture the whole both in its organic unity and in the perfection of all portions of the book. The Scriptures, comprising Moses and the prophets and the Psalms (Luke 24:44) alongside the gospel narrative (Galatians 3:8; Romans 16:26) and the writings of the apostles (2 Peter 3:16) are the testimony of the Lord Jesus Christ (John 5:39). If then we have in Scripture a full and adequate testimony of Christ, who but the divine Spirit of God could be the Author? The world did not understand Christ because He was from heaven. How could they if they did not know Him? Not even Paul, regenerated by divine revelation and the indwelling Spirit, could say that he knew Him, but that he desired to know Him (Philippians 3:10). Whatever knowledge Paul had was by the Spirit. The more the supremacy of the Holy Spirit is acknowledged, the more the Word is fixed in our heart. God's Words are not merely letters. They are spirit and life. They are not only a power to be felt but a voice to be heard (See Acts 15:28; 1 Corinthians 14:36,37).

If the work of the Holy Spirit is to enlighten minds and renew hearts, then His special work towards men is the Scriptures. A consideration of the Old Testament writings reveals that it was not the meditation of the writers that elevated them to see marvellous and future things - it was the Spirit of the eternal God that came upon them. "Thus saith the LORD", said the prophets. Again, "The mouth of the LORD hath spoken it" (Isaiah 58:14).

Nor are those expressions confined to the Old Testament writings. In every age of development of the Scriptures "men spake from God being moved by the Holy Spirit" (2 Peter 1:21). If the gospels had been written by man's recall rather than by being God-breathed, how could they adequately describe the life of Jesus Christ and His profound sayings, so perfect in every expression? How could men, of themselves, adequately write of events unseen, such as Christ's temptation in the wilderness? The character of their presentation: Matthew describing Him as Messiah, King, Mark as the perfect Servant, Luke as Son of Man and John as Son of God, produces a divine wholeness of which man's thought is incapable. The Spirit of God alone can give adequate representation of the life of Christ. As we enter the epistles we find for instance, that in Hebrews both quotations and the drawing out of an important truth are attributed to the Holy Spirit (Matthew 3:7; 9:8).

How, then, did this all come about? Let us focus attention on a few key passages of Scripture. These are 2 Timothy 3:16; 1 Peter 1:10; 2 Peter 1:21. We must differentiate clearly between inspired men, as some are sometimes described, and the inspired or God-breathed writings. We do not rest our faith on men. With the inspired Word we rest our faith on a divine testimony, believing that it is received from God (1 Thessalonians 2:13).

It is evident from the passages of Scripture referred to above that the Holy Spirit and not their own spirit revealed to chosen men what they wrote. Their writings, they confessed, were high above their own measure of spiritual insight. Men spoke (and wrote) from God, being moved by the Holy Spirit. The Spirit that was in them was the Spirit of Christ, testifying to Him. He revealed to them what they did not understand although they searched and enquired about it. See 1 Peter 1:11 in this respect. David said, "The Spirit of the LORD spake by me" (2 Samuel 23:2). David was aware of expressions of thought too lofty for him to generate or to grasp. Peter testified to the Spirit's words through David when he said, "it was needful that the scripture should be fulfilled, which the Holy Spirit spake before by the mouth of David" (Acts 1:10).

Yet, how wonderful are the ways of God! How marvellous that the Spirit's work in forming the Scriptures took account of man's individuality, history and experience. Job wrote in very ancient times; Moses was skilled in Egypt's wisdom; Amos was a humble shepherd; Daniel was a statesman in Babylon; Peter was a fisherman; Paul wrote in times of Roman authority. Throughout, the Spirit used the circumstances, natural endowment and experience of men in His work.

Being Spirit-given, the Scriptures are an eternal book, a record of the past and a guide for the present and future. The inspiration of

Scripture through the Holy Spirit extends to its very form of expression. As perfect harmony in music includes the silent pause, so the divine Composer has enlightened our minds by what is not spoken as well as by what is spoken. For example, silence in Genesis about Melchizedek's genealogy is used later to emphasize the everlasting nature of the priesthood of the Lord. Other gems appear. Peter's experience at Joppa when he fell into a trance emphasizes for us how the gracious Spirit was prepared to take up Peter's physical and mental state to reveal precious truth. This was not something Peter had dreamt up. Peter learned from his experience that the blessing of God in salvation is universal.

It is clear from the Revised Standard Version of 2 Timothy 3:16, not that Scripture WAS inspired but that it IS inspired. We are listening to the voice of God as often as we read. The Spirit has breathed here and in no other book. It is the Word proceeding out of the mouth of God. In obeying its precepts we know that we are acting in obedience to our heavenly Father.

Being Spirit-given, the Scriptures are an eternal book, a record of the past and a guide for the present and future. Being written by the Spirit through men, it cannot fulfil its purpose in our lives except by the continual guidance and blessing of the self-same Spirit. It requires a quickened heart and an exercised conscience. In general, books may present things logically and imaginatively, addressing conscience and feeling, but Scripture alone speaks to the whole man - to "all that is within" (See Psalm 103:1). This penetrating power is another feature of its divine origin.

How impossible for the unspiritual man to understand God-breathed words! Men may understand the structures of the book, its grammar, its language, but they cannot understand the soul of Scripture. It is spiritually discerned, the Psalmist said, "Open Thou mine eyes" (Psalm 119:18).

How striking is the unity of Scripture and how impossible to account for it, considering the diversity of the authors, unless we realize that all Scripture is one great organic whole, possessed of the same spirit and life, inspired by the holy Spirit who knows the end of all things from the beginning.

The testimony which so solemnly concludes the book of Revelation we believe can be viewed as having reference to all Scripture. "If any man shall add unto it, God shall add unto him the plagues which are written in this book: And if any man shall take away from the words of the book of this prophecy, God shall take away his part from the tree of life, and out of the holy city, which are written in this book" (Revelation 22:18,19).

Solemn words! "Now unto Him that is able to do exceeding abundantly above all that we ask or think, according to the power that worketh in us, unto Him be the glory in the Church and in Christ Jesus unto all generations for ever and ever. Amen" (Ephesians 3:20,21).

CHAPTER THREE: OLD TESTAMENT ACTIVITIES OF THE HOLY SPIRIT (JIM SEDDON)

"Not by might, nor by power, but by My Spirit, saith the LORD." These words of Zechariah 4:6, reflect the truth that the Holy Spirit is active in relation to all the purposes of the triune God. From Genesis 1:2 we learn that "the earth was waste and void; and darkness was upon the face of the deep; and the Spirit of God moved upon the face of the waters". Thus began His preparatory work for the creation of an environment in which would dwell man, who would be the supreme object of His love and grace and experience a relationship with his God that no other creature could know.

This relationship was marred through the disobedience of Adam, yet the Spirit of God was ever active to restore that relationship, and to make known the divine purposes of God in man. "My Spirit shall not strive with man for ever" (Genesis 6:3). Yet in His grace, He strove long and hard, and what was true of Israel was true of the whole of mankind before them.

"Yet many years didst Thou bear with them and testified against them through Thy prophets" (Nehemiah 9:30). "Searching what time or what manner of time the Spirit of Christ which was in them did point unto, when it (He) testified beforehand the sufferings of Christ, and the glories that should follow them" (1 Peter 1:11).

Applying Peter's words to the activity of the Holy Spirit in the individual saint of God in the Old Testament, reveals His beautiful work of foreshadowing the lovely Person of our Lord Jesus Christ. Perhaps Joseph was the most comprehensive example of them all: his whole life, through the Spirit of God, typified the Lord Jesus: His unique relationship with his father (Genesis 37:3); the hatred of his brethren towards him; the sufferings he endured as the sent one (Psalm 105:17-19); his exaltation from the prison house to be Lord over all Egypt and become Zaphenath-paneah (saviour of the world). Truly we see the work of the Holy Spirit as expressed by Pharaoh when he said "Can we find such a one as this, a man in whom the Spirit of God is?" (Genesis 41:38).

From one generation to another the Holy Spirit was working out the divine purposes of God. Prominent among them was that He should have a people among whom He could dwell. In the midst of that people He put His Holy Spirit (Isaiah 63:11) who was to empower men and women for the building of God's dwelling.

> "And Moses said unto the children of Israel, See the LORD has called by name Bezalel ... and He hath filled him with the Spirit of God, in wisdom, in understanding, and in knowledge, and in all manner of workmanship" (Exodus 35:30,31).

Thus from the time they left Egypt, and through all their wilderness journey, "Thou gavest also Thy good Spirit to instruct them" (Nehemiah 9:20), raising up leaders for them. "And the LORD said unto Moses, Gather unto Me seventy men of the elders of

Israel - and I will take of the Spirit which is upon thee, and will put it (Him) upon them" (Numbers 11:16,17).

The purpose of the Spirit of God was to guide them into all the blessings He had in store for them, but how often they tried His longsuffering grace, proving they were no better than the nations from whom God had separated them. "But they rebelled and grieved His Holy Spirit: therefore He was turned to be their enemy, and Himself fought against them" (Isaiah 63:10). The result of this leads us into the sad days of the Judges. The persecution and oppression by their enemies bore witness to the people's departure from God.

> "And the Spirit of the LORD came upon him, and he judged Israel, and he went out to war, and the LORD delivered" (Judges 3:10).

Whenever they cried to the Lord, confessing their sin, and acknowledging their dependence upon Him, He raised up men who through His Spirit delivered them. As Judges records, when they "cried unto the LORD, the LORD raised up a saviour to the children of Israel, who saved them, even Othniel ... and the Spirit of the LORD came upon him, and he judged Israel" (Judges 3:9,10). Gideon too, God raised up to be their saviour from the Midianites, through the power of the Holy Spirit. "Then all the Midianites and the Amalekites and the children of the east assembled themselves together; and they passed over, and pitched in the valley of Jezreel, but the Spirit of the LORD came upon Gideon" (Judges 6:33,34).

The writer to the Hebrews lists such individuals of whom it was said that the Spirit of God came upon them, men and women who were among the great worthies of Scripture. "And what shall I more say? For the time will fail me if I tell of Gideon, Barak, Samson, Jephthah" (Hebrews 11:32). Yet in spite of all the long-suffering of the Holy Spirit, the book of the Judges closes with this sad indictment: "In those days there was no king in Israel: every man did that which was right in his own eyes" (Judges 21:25).

"And the Spirit of God came mightily upon him, and he prophesied among them" (1 Samuel 10:10).

From the judges to the kings, the activity of the Holy Spirit is clearly seen raising up men to carry out the will of God. The words quoted above were in reference to the anointing of Saul to be the first king of Israel, but like so many before him, he grieved the Spirit of God, who departed from him. Saul sowed the seed of disobedience, and he reaped the fruit of rejection (see 1 Samuel 16:14). But in contrast the Lord "raised up David to be their king; to whom also He bare witness, and said, I have found David the son of Jesse, a man after My heart, who shall do all My will" (Acts13:22).

Such words spoken by God stand out in contrast to those spoken by the children of Israel when they said, "Make us a king to judge us like all the nations" (1 Samuel 8:5), and Saul proved to be the people's man. But David was God's man, God's choice, and was to mark him out as such, for we read, "Then Samuel took the horn of oil, and anointed him in the midst of his brethren" (1 Samuel 16:13).

David's life revealed much of the Spirit's activities, manifesting not only His power, but much of His love and grace also. He knew in great measure what it was not only to live by the Spirit, but by the Spirit also to walk (Galatians 5:25). David was the author of at least 66 of the 150 Psalms, the work of inspiration through the Spirit of God. His appreciation of his dependence upon the Holy Spirit is seen not only in his office as king of Israel, but more important still, in his relationship and communion with God. This is expressed in the words he wrote, "Cast me not away from Thy presence; and take not Thy Holy Spirit from me" (Psalm 51:11). The sin in David's life caused him to realize the sad possibility of the Holy Spirit being taken from him. While this cannot be so in the case of a believer today (John 14:16), nevertheless sin can grieve Him and quench His work in us.

The divine record sums up the life of the "sweet psalmist of Israel", the "man after His own heart" with the words, "And he died in a good old age, full of days, riches, and honour" (1 Chronicles 29:28). So, on through the Old Testament the Holy Spirit continued to speak to the people of God through His prophets, yet they still rebelled, in spite of all His loving entreaties, until eventually God's earthly dwelling was destroyed, and His people led away into captivity, and for seventy years they remained in Babylon.

But the longing of God was still for His people among whom He could dwell, so the Spirit of God moved in the hearts of a remnant, and they returned to rebuild His house. For some five hundred years He persevered with them, until the coming of the Lord Jesus. When the old dispensation gives place to the new, the Holy Spirit manifests the grace of God to the whole of mankind, convicting "the world in respect of sin, and of righteousness, and of judgement" (John 16:8). Having been sent from the Father (John 15:26), the Holy Spirit is working towards the consummation of the great purpose of the age, "The Church, which is His Body" (Ephesians 1:22,23). Marvellous grace indeed!

May He, the blessed Paraclete,

Who with us doth abide

God's gracious purpose to complete,

Be day by day our Guide.

CHAPTER FOUR: THE HOLY SPIRIT IN CHRIST ON EARTH (ALEX REID)

Was there even a moment in the life of the Lord Jesus Christ when the Holy Spirit did not fill Him? Clearly not! The eternal Son of God became the Son of Man at the fulness of the time when God sent Him forth. Matthew 1:20 says of Mary, "that which has been conceived in her is of the Holy Spirit". Luke quotes the words of the angel to Mary when he says: "The Holy Spirit will come upon you, and the power of the Most High will overshadow you" (1:35). The conception of the Lord was a miracle of Deity, completely unique, and a cooperation of the three Persons of the Godhead. Both humility and majesty are seen in that unique Baby: unable to speak, yet Himself the Word; unable to feed Himself, yet the Bread of Life that whoever comes to Him should never hunger; unable to fend for Himself, yet come to save His people and the whole world from their sins!

When, thirty three days after the Lord's circumcision Mary brought her offerings to the Lord according to Leviticus 12:8, she presented Jesus to the Lord (Luke 2:22). The testimony of God through Simeon was: "And it had been revealed to him by the Holy Spirit that he would not see death before he had seen the Lord's Christ" (v.26). No wonder Simeon blessed God as he took this Child in his arms! Mary and Joseph were amazed at the things being said, yet the Spirit was making it clear that this Child was none other than God in the flesh.

As Jesus grew, He was always doing the business of His heavenly Father, though subject to His earthly parents. He kept increasing in wisdom and stature, and in favor with God and men (Luke 2:49-52), proof of the Spirit's testimony about His identity and evidence of the Spirit's power within Him. His later testimony about Himself was "He who sent Me is with Me; He has not left Me alone, for I always do the things that are pleasing to Him" (John 8:29). It was not simply that He never displeased the Father, but rather that He always pleased Him in everything He thought or said or did! So Paul writes about the Spirit-filled life of the follower of the Lord, "walk by the Spirit, and you will not carry out the desire of the flesh ... if we live by the Spirit, let us also walk by the Spirit" (Galatians 5:16, 25). The Lord is the perfect example.

Evidence of the pleasure of the Father is seen clearly at His baptism where, according to Luke 3:22, "the Holy Spirit descended upon Him in bodily form like a dove, and a voice came out of heaven, Thou art My beloved Son, in Thee I am well-pleased". The first thirty years of His life had pleased His Father well; so now too did His public ministry.

Paul commands the Ephesians to "be filled with the Spirit" (Ephesians 5:18). The disciple must walk in the same manner as He walked (1 John 2:6) and it is clear that the Master was full of the Spirit. In Luke 4:1, 2 we read: "And Jesus, full of the Holy Spirit, returned from the Jordan and was led about by the Spirit in the wilderness for forty days, being tempted by the devil". We would naturally prefer to avoid that kind of exposure to the devil's wiles. Yet this perfect One did not resist the Holy Spirit as did those before Him and those who would come after Him (Acts

7:51). He did not quench the Spirit, something His disciples today must not do either (1 Thessalonians 5:19). In his responses
to the devil, lie did not grieve the Spirit, the perfect example of
the commanded response of the present day disciple (Ephesians
4:30).

We read in Galatians 5:22 that joy is one of the aspects of the
fruit of the Spirit, which fruit was seen clearly in the life of the
Lord Jesus. Though he was in a state of physical starvation, His
strength came from the Spirit of God. No one who is full of the
Spirit sins (1 John 3:6); conversely, one who sins cannot be full
of the Spirit. In the greatest temptation that any man ever faced,
this perfect Man resisted the devil, and the devil departed from
Him. Perhaps it was with this in view that James wrote to disciples of the Lord and said, "Resist the devil and he will flee from
you. Draw near to God and He will draw near to you" (James
4:7, 8). The Lord said, "... the ruler of the world is coming, and
he has nothing in Me" (John 14:30). No wonder this One makes
such a sympathetic high priest today in the presence of God! He
"has been tempted in all things as we are, yet without sin" (Hebrews 4:15). What marvellous evidence of the power of the Holy
Spirit!

Luke goes on to tell how the Lord, after the devil had finished
every temptation, "returned to Galilee in the power of the Spirit"
(Luke 4:14). It was in that power that He opened the book in
the synagogue in Nazareth, his home town, and read: "The Spirit
of the Lord is upon Me, because He anointed Me to preach the
gospel to the poor. Today this Scripture has been fulfilled in your
hearing" (Luke 4:18, 21).

They began to speak well of him and wonder "at the gracious words which were falling from his lips", no doubt an evidence of the power of the Spirit. Within minutes, however, they were about to throw Him down a cliff, so outraged were they at what lie had then said. "But passing through their midst, He went His way" (4:30); a different evidence of the power of the Spirit, not only that lie avoided them, but, still gracious, that He did not destroy them with a word.

Paul declared of his own ministry to the Gentiles that it was sanctified by the Holy Spirit, and that what was accomplished through him was in the power of the Spirit (Romans 15:16,19). Indeed, that was a fulfilment of the Lord's own words to His disciples in Matthew 10:20, "For it is not you who speak, but it is the Spirit of your Father who speaks in you". That was the power in which the Lord spoke as well. John the Baptist referred to the Lord and said: "For He whom God has sent speaks the words of God; for He [God] gives the Spirit without measure" (John 3:34).

With a word, He cast out demons by the Spirit of God (Matthew 12:28). So he could confidently explain to His disciples that when they were in trouble, "the Holy Spirit will teach you in that very hour what you ought to say" (Luke 12:12). Not only did the Lord have the Spirit without measure, but His own disciples had and are to have the same as well (compare Titus 3:5,6). It is no surprise then to see Stephen, a man full of the Spirit, confounding men with the wisdom and the Spirit with which he was speaking (Acts 6).

Paul writes to the Romans and says: "But if anyone does not have the Spirit of Christ, he does not belong to Him" (Romans 8:9). What a testimony to the presence and power of the Holy Spirit of God resident in the person of Jesus Christ, that lie is seen to be equally the Spirit of Christ and the Spirit of God.

Luke 10:21 records that, upon the return of the seventy commissioned preachers of the Word of the Lord, and their delight that even the spirits were subject to them in the name of the Lord, "At that very time He rejoiced greatly in the Holy Spirit", and praised His Father. Even His joy was motivated by the presence of the Spirit within Him. We read in Galatians 5:22 that joy is one of the aspects of the fruit of the Spirit, which fruit was seen clearly in the life of the Lord Jesus.

Another evidence of the fulness of the Spirit in the Lord is seen in Luke 5:16: "But He Himself would often slip away to the wilderness and pray" (e.g. Matthew 14:23; Mark 1:35; Luke 6:12). It is clear from a comparison of scripture with scripture that this was not so that lie might be filled with the Spirit, but as rather a result of that fulness (see also Jude 20). As He was God the Son, unity with the Father and the Spirit compelled Him to pray. What depth and power were in His prayer! One marvels at the depth of the communication that took place in the garden of Gethsemane when the Lord Jesus prayed about His imminent crucifixion: "And being in agony He was praying very fervently; and his sweat became like drops of blood, falling down upon the ground" (Luke 22:44).

Was any prayer of the Lord not fervent? Yet here particularly His prayer was very fervent because of His agony of soul. No long-windedness or vain repetition here. The result was "not My will, but Thine be done". How could anyone but a Spirit-filled Man speak such words in the face of such torment!

His Spirit-led walk took Him to the Cross, where through the eternal Spirit, He would offer Himself without blemish to God: the eternal Son, offering Himself to the eternal God through the eternal Spirit. As there was a miracle of Deity at His birth, completely unique and a cooperation of the three Persons of the Godhead, so also was there the same thing at His death. The Holy Spirit, present at His baptism at the Jordan was also present at that straightening baptism at Calvary where the Lord Jesus offered Himself without blemish to God by means of (Greek: dia) the eternal Spirit (Hebrews 9:14). Yet the means by which Christ offered Himself was not available in this one instance for companionship, comfort, communion. The Lord shared the agony of the Cross with no one (cf. Psalm 22:1,2; 102:6,7). Nonetheless, it was through the Spirit of God that Jesus was raised from the dead (Romans 8:11).

What delight to consider the Lord on earth, One who was anointed by God "with the Holy Spirit and with power" (Acts 10:38).

CHAPTER FIVE: THE SPIRITUAL GIFTS OF THE HOLY SPIRIT (ROY DICKSON)

The Scriptures clearly teach that each individual member of the Church the Body of Christ is given a spiritual gift, for we read in 1 Corinthians 12:6,7, "there are diversities of workings, but the same God, who worketh all things in all. But to each one is given the manifestation of the Spirit to profit." Those gifts were primarily meant to find their expression within churches of God and the purpose of this chapter is to develop Scriptural examples of some of those gifts and to encourage personal identification and diligent exercise of such gifts.

The Purpose of the Gifts

Spiritual gifts are specifically dealt with in five places in the New Testament: Romans 12:3-8; 1 Corinthians 12:4-1 1; Ephesians 4:7-12 and 1 Peter 4:10,11. Some gifts were given to fulfil God's special purposes at the beginning of this present dispensation in the establishing and development of the churches of God, and were often associated with miraculous power as evidence of God's presence in their midst. Other gifts continue to find expression today and are the manifestation of the Spirit's presence in the believer. These gifts are given, that in both personal and corporate testimony, we might know the Spirit's blessing in our work for the Lord.

As we develop our subject it is necessary to give a Scriptural definition of the word "gift". The Greek word used in passages noted above, and elsewhere, is charisma meaning, "grace, favour, kindness" (Young). We can see, therefore, that the bestowal of such a gift is entirely God's prerogative. We have no right to question His decisions in these matters, but we do have a responsibility to discern and develop whatever gifts we have been given.

We are stewards and have been given responsibility to use our spiritual gifts to our Master's benefit and glory, knowing that one day we shall stand before Him to answer to Him as to how we traded on His behalf.

In 1 Peter 4:10 we read, "According as each hath received a gift, ministering it among yourselves, as good stewards of the manifold grace of God". We note, first of all, that the principle is, "according as a man hath, not according as he hath not" (2 Corinthians 8:12), for God holds us responsible for what He has entrusted to our care. That is why Peter refers to those who are, "good stewards of the manifold grace of God". We are stewards and have been given responsibility to use our spiritual gifts to our Master's benefit and glory, knowing that one day we shall stand before Him to answer to Him as to how we "traded" on His behalf.

There are two passages in the New Testament where, in each case the Lord Jesus Christ tells the parable of a man going to a far country, who before leaving, calls his servants to instruct them as to their responsibilities in his absence. It is interesting to note that in Matthew 25:15 we read that the servants were given varying amounts of money, "to each according to his several ability", whereas in Luke 19:13 the ten servants each received an identical amount of money, but each being given the commandment, "Trade ye herewith till I come".

There seems to be a powerful lesson here in respect of the gifts we receive from God. In Matthew the Lord would teach, and it is self-evident, that we cannot expect, nor do we all have, the same gifts and responsibilities in our spiritual service for God. In Luke He is clearly demonstrating, as we noted in I Corinthians 12:7, that all believers have been given gifts which they are personally responsible to exercise. All will one day answer to the Lord Jesus as to how they used their gifts during His absence. Solemn thought indeed! But we should take encouragement from the fact that in both passages faithful service brought the commendation, "Well done". So Peter exhorts his readers in the matter of "ministering" their gifts. The word for ministering is the Greek word diakoneo meaning to act as a deacon, or to serve, the emphasis being on the work to be done rather than the relationship between lord and servant. Thus we see that there is a God-given responsibility to minister our gifts amongst the people of God.

The Variety of the Gifts

What gifts should we expect to see manifest today? The five main passages previously noted give Scriptural examples of the gifts we should expect to see manifested in the Church the Body and more particularly amongst the people of God. In Romans 12:6-8 Paul deals with four gifts:

> 1. Prophecy - literally "the speaking forth of the mind and counsel of God" (Vine). This is not the same as prophecy which was received by the apostles and

prophets as being the revealed word of God in some particular matter, but rather the delivering of a message from God as a result of prayer and meditation upon the Scriptures.

2. Ministry - envisages the work of serving in the exposition of the Word, for example Acts 6:4, but also carries the thought of compassionate love towards others finding expression in practical service to their needs, as in deacon service.

3. Teaching - to give instruction. The word is used some 95 times in the New Testament. Paul says to Timothy regarding certain matters, "These things command and teach" (1 Timothy 4:11).

4. Exhorting - the word means to call on, entreat or encourage. Paul exhorts us to pray for all men, as in 1 Timothy 2:1. The writer to the Hebrews speaks of the need for daily encouragement (Hebrews 3:13). Of course, those who encourage need to ensure that their lives measure up to what they are encouraging others to do.

Gifts noted in the other passages include 1 Corinthians 12:28:

1. Teachers - those able to handle aright the Word of truth (2 Timothy 2:15).

2. Helps - giving assistance, particularly to the weak and needy (Vine).

3. Governments - the work of oversight under the direction and control of the Holy Spirit (see Acts 20:28).

We have already referred to 1 Peter 4 when looking at ministering our gifts. Specifically in verses 9-11, however, Peter refers to:

1. Using hospitality - literally a lover of strangers. See also 1 Timothy 3:2 and Titus 1:8.

2. Speaking the oracles of God speaking God's utterances.

3. Ministering as of the strength which God supplieth - serving with the strength that God gives.

Discerning and Using our Gifts

We now need to challenge our own hearts firstly to identify what our gifts might be and secondly as to their use and development in Christian service. Solomon tells us, "A man's gift maketh room for Him, and bringeth him before great men" (Proverbs 18:16). We have previously noted that we all, brethren and sisters, receive a gift through the indwelling Holy Spirit. Brethren have the opportunity and responsibility to exercise their gifts by leading in prayer and worship within the context of service in the house of God. Sisters learn to exercise their gifts in subjection to their brethren. However, no matter which assembly with which we are linked, no matter whether there are few or many on the assembly roll, there is a work of God for us all to do.

One of the gifts we noted in Romans 12:8 was that of exhorting. This is a gift we can all be exercised about, particularly in the matter of exhorting each other in the use of our individual gifts from the Lord, for we all need encouragement in the work of the Lord. Within the local assembly overseers have a responsibility to discern gift among the saints and encourage its use and development. The apostle Paul look a great personal interest in the spiritual development of a young man called Timothy. His words to Timothy should be of encouragement to us all no matter what our age or spiritual experience. "Neglect not the gift that is in thee. Be diligent in these things; give thyself wholly to them; that thy progress may be manifest unto all" (1 Timothy 4:14,15); then he adds in verse 16, 'Take heed to thyself, and to thy teaching. Continue in these things; for in doing this thou shalt save both thyself and them that hear thee".

Finally, in all that we do, or may be exercised to do for the Lord, we need to have a prayer burden. Romans 12:3 makes it clear that we need to make a realistic assessment of our abilities for it is "according as God hath dealt to each man a measure of faith". Our brethren and sisters can give helpful encouragement but ultimately we need to know the Spirit's leading through prayer.

CHAPTER SIX: OLD TESTAMENT EMBLEMS OF THE HOLY SPIRIT (GREG NEELY)

When the apostle John wished to communicate to his readers the idea of the incarnation of Christ, that the Lord had become a real man with a real body having real substance, he put it in the following words: "That which we have heard, that which we have seen with our eyes, that which we beheld, and our hands handled, concerning the Word of life" (1 John 1:1). The key words are heard, seen, beheld and handled.

He was describing the physical experience of seeing and touching the Lord: an experience only possible when confronted by a real man having substance and form. The same things could not have been written of the Holy Spirit, for He is invisible to the eye and cannot be touched or handled by human hands. This is because the Spirit has no physical form or substance. Therefore the emblems employed in the Old Testament to convey the idea of the Person of the Spirit, must present the thought of formless fluidity, yet at the same time portraying presence and activity. Emblems of the Spirit are therefore things like oil; fire; smoke; wind; rain etc. For the purpose of this chapter we will limit ourselves to two Old Testament emblems: oil and the pillar of fire and cloud.

Oil

Olive oil was the substance used in the lamps mounted on the lampstand in the Tabernacle (Exodus 27:20) and for a number of other purposes in the Old Testament. But before we touch on those, we must first try to show from Scripture what leads us to think that oil is an emblem of the Holy Spirit.

In Zechariah 4, the principal thought being conveyed to Zerubbabel through the prophetic vision is that the Spirit of God is active, and it is His activity, not human resolve, that will bring to fruition the work of God (v.6). This is communicated in a vision of oil lamps on a lampstand, being fed from a central reservoir, which is in turn fed by two olive trees or branches. We are told in v.14 that the two olive trees represent two people; the oil which proceeds from the trees (v.12) represents the Spirit of God and the light of the lamps the Spirit fed testimony being borne to Zerubbabel and the people of those days. This interpretation of Zechariah's vision, that the lamps, oil and trees represent the testimony of the Spirit of God through human agency, would seem to be supported by reference to Revelation 11:4, where two prophetic witnesses of a future time are described as: "The two olive trees and the two lampstands" (RVM).

Having established that oil in the Old Testament is emblematic of the Spirit, we can now look at various uses of oil in Scripture, which will show us different aspects of the Spirit's work. The children of Israel were commanded to bring pure olive oil to fuel the lamps that lit the interior of the Tabernacle (Exodus 27:20). The purpose of the burning lamps on their stands was to "give light in front of the lampstand" (Numbers 8:2; Exodus 25:37). The lamps thus illuminated the interior of the tent and the other furnishings in it. This brings to our minds the Spirit's work in illuminating the minds of believers, relative to the truths and services of the house of God and things related to the Person and work of the Lord Jesus. This is what Christ Himself taught His disciples to expect when the Spirit was sent forth:

> "Howbeit when He, the Spirit of truth is come, He shall guide you into all the truth ... He shall glorify Me: for He shall take of Mine, and shall declare it unto you" (John 16:12-14).

In the use of oil as one of the ingredients of the meal offering, we have a picture of the Holy Spirit in association with the life of the Lord. In Leviticus 2:4, we have described for us two ways of bringing together the flour and oil of the meal offering; it was either, "Unleavened cakes of fine flour mingled with oil, or unleavened wafers anointed with oil". The mingling of the flour and oil meant that the one was totally absorbed by the other, speaking to us of the complete yielding by Christ to the leading of the Spirit. The Lord's words and actions were so in harmony with the will of the Spirit of God, that it would be impossible to distinguish the two, just as it would be impossible to separate the oil and flour once mixed. This glorious unity of the Son and Spirit is indicated to us by Luke: "And Jesus, full of the Holy Spirit, returned from the Jordan, and was led by the Spirit in the wilderness" (Luke 4:1). The anointing of the unleavened wafer (Leviticus 2:4) would speak of the Lord's anointing with the Spirit that marked Him out as God's chosen Servant (cf. Isaiah 61:1; Luke 4:18).

What did the Lord mean by the words: "Lo, I am with you alway, even unto the end of the world"? He meant that He would be with them in the Person of the Spirit. The abiding presence of the Holy Spirit was their assurance that He was with them in their mission.

The Pillar of Fire and Cloud

The second emblem to be considered is the pillar of fire and cloud (See Exodus 13:21-22; Nehemiah 9:12, 19). There seem to have been two main purposes connected with this pillar. They were: to assure the people of Israel that God's presence was with them, that He had not forsaken them, and to be a guide for them in their wilderness journey, "to lead them in the way" (Nehemiah 9:19).

When the Lord Jesus on the mountain in Galilee, had delivered to His disciples the great commission of going into all the nations to teach, baptize and make new disciples, He assured them that He would be present with them even to the end of the world (Matthew 28:16-20). He said this knowing that shortly He would take His leave of them and they would see Him no more. So what did the Lord mean by the words: "Lo, I am with you alway, even unto the end of the world"? He meant that He would be with them in the Person of the Spirit.

The abiding presence of the Holy Spirit was their assurance that He was with them in their mission. The words, "Even unto the end of the world [or 'age' RV margin]", indicate to us that this promise was not only applicable to those who stood with Christ that day, but to all who would become His disciples in the unfolding age of grace. This thought is confirmed to us in the writings of the beloved disciple when he recorded the Lord's words: "He shall give you another Comforter ... even the Spirit of truth

... for He abideth with you, and shall be in you. I will not leave you desolate: I come unto you" (John 14:16-18).

During Israel's wilderness journey, the pillar of fire and cloud was their guide, indicating not only where they should journey to, but determining also their length of stay (See Numbers 9:15-23). In the New Testament the Holy Spirit is seen as the heavenly guide in the lives of believers; not only in the sense of leading them into an understanding of spiritual truth, as we have already considered, but also leading and guiding in the outworking of spiritual principles in daily life and service for God. The apostles Peter and Paul experienced the direct guiding of the Spirit in their labours for the Master, each of them receiving specific instruction from the Spirit as to where they should and should not go (See Acts 10:19, 20; 13:2-4; 16:10). Through prayer, practical guidance from the Spirit as to where and in what our sphere of service should lie, is available to the believer today. Also, in our daily wrestling against our old nature, it is the guidance and leading of the Spirit that will steer our everyday conduct away from the lusts of the flesh (See Galatians 5:16, 18, 25) into an enjoyment of the fruit of the Spirit (Galatians 5:22).

CHAPTER SEVEN: A HABITATION OF GOD IN THE SPIRIT (BRIAN FULLARTON)

The one great aim of every New Testament letter is to reveal the amazing purpose of God in His Son, Jesus Christ and the working out of that purpose through the Holy Spirit. Early on the page of divine record we find the Spirit of God "moved upon the face of the waters"; He "hovered" with a view to finding a resting-place. This has ever been the divine desire. A series of momentous events follow: light, separation, gathering together, rule and productivity. These have a spiritual counterpart in the outworking of the divine will (compare Genesis 1:2,6,9,16 and 20 with 2 Corinthians 6:14-18) for the present era of grace.

Background

The historical narrative brings us to Exodus 25:8,9 in the expression of the Eternal for a dwelling place among His people "Let them make Me a sanctuary ... according to the pattern of the Tabernacle" (Hebrew: dwelling). God gave the plan, the people had to build. The Temple, which filled the heart of David, was built by Solomon. It was a house of habitation for God to dwell in. He would come down and fill such with His glory (1 Kings 8:13; 9:3). The Temple was to be a place of prayer, justice and worship. His demand upon His people was separation from all others (1 Kings 8:53).

The Current Plan

Every believer is sealed with the Holy Spirit at the moment of salvation. His incoming and indwelling presence is a work of divine ownership upon the believer. His work, following that wonderful experience, is to reveal God's will for the life of service and He alone is able to impart the ability to do just what is pleasing to Him who called us by His grace. This development is seen in three particular passages highlighting the Spirit's presence in believers together, holding the pattern of New Testament teaching concerning churches of God forming the house of God. They are:

> 1. 1 Corinthians 3:16,17 - emphasizing the Sanctity of God's dwelling place.

> 2. Ephesians 2:20-22 - with accent on the Unity of His dwelling place.

> 3. 1 Peter 2:10 - underlining Service within His dwelling place.

So, we are dealing with the Spirit's presence in the corporate structure of the house of God expressed in the term "a holy temple", "a habitation of God" and "a spiritual house".

1 Corinthians 3

The application of the building metaphor is applied to the Church of God in Corinth (v.9). A building is not an organic structure in itself. It is composed of stones, bricks and mortar, bonded together to form a whole. The materials themselves and their arrangement must conform to a pattern of structure. The same principles apply in the spiritual sphere. The apostle uses the term "temple" (Greek: 'naos' - inner shrine) to convey the truth of the distinctive position of the Church of God in Corinth being a sanctified dwelling place of the Spirit of God, a holy community by virtue of the disciples' association with and obedience to the Lord. The Spirit of God was "in" the saints as a collective expression of those gathered to His Name and keeping His Word.

His deity is attested in His title. "Know ye not" is not simply the knowledge of a doctrine, but the appreciation of fact that a divine, living Person inhabited this shrine which must conform to His nature and character. Human pride, worldly wisdom and earthly defilement have no place there. His personal indwelling is not to be considered a merely abstract concept. He endows blessing and enriches experience where His presence is acknowledged. The Church in Corinth was not one of many temples (temple is singular, ye is plural in v.16 RV) but formed part of the one Temple of God consisting of churches of God bonded together in the Lord (see Ephesians 2:21). The absence of the article, in the Greek, before temple (1 Corinthians 3:16) indicates its character as a fitting residence, being built according to the divine pattern given by the Holy Spirit. This must be differentiated from 1 Corinthians 6:19 which has to do with the unconditional and abiding presence of the Spirit in the believer's body. Like the truth of the individual's dwelling, the corporate unit of testimony is to glorify God and not give expression to self-pleasing attitudes.

"Ye are not your own"

The Spirit's presence in any golden lampstand holds no guarantee of permanence where He is not allowed to live as He would and is forced to leave. In the past, Israel amongst whom God dwelt, both in the Tabernacle and later in the Temple, defiled themselves by idolatry and were judged, by God. They were to illuminate His splendour and glory, which they will do yet again when His habitation will be amongst men (Jeremiah 31:33). Carnal conduct and false teaching mar and can destroy God's testimony. Christ's glory is not to be diminished by moral defilement or doctrinal error. The work done in the Temple of God is to be of qualitative and quantitative value. We are to think reverently and practically about this gracious, holy, almighty Person from whom we receive nourishment and by whom we achieve spiritual advancement. His acquaintance should be cultivated.

Ephesians 2

Again, we come across the word naos, the inner sanctuary, corresponding to the holy of holies in Tabernacle and Temple in v.21 of Ephesians 2. The term "household (adjective - belonging to the house) of God" denotes not the family of God but the house of God with the focus on standing and service within the house, consistent with the temple imagery underlying vv.20-22. These verses reach a high level of spiritual knowledge, a summit of divinely revealed truth regarding the purpose of God for believers in service together. From the graveyard of sin at the commencement of the chapter, we are brought to God's dwelling-place at the end, through Him who is not only our peace, the unifying bond between the divided parties of Jews and Gentiles, but who is also the Chief Corner Stone of the spiritual house.

The foundation (v.20) is that laid by the apostles and prophets not the men themselves. No such prominence is given to men. No other foundation than Christ (see 1 Cor. 3:10-11) and His teaching, given during the forty days of Acts 1:3. The apostles and prophets fulfilled their purpose and, like the sign-gifts of early New Testament times, are no longer with us, their day of usefulness having come to an end but their teaching is embodied in "the Faith" (Jude 3) for the day of grace. Christ is the unifying bond of the Body and also the uniting stone of the spiritual temple, He is the integral and essential part, securing position and giving unity to the whole structure.

The holy temple is described "in the Lord" (v.21), not "in Christ". The latter refers to our heavenly position in spiritual union, with our Saviour, the former to early testimony in spiritual association with others who own Him as Lord, in subjection to His will. The one Temple (v.21) comprises every church of God (every building, cp. 1 Cor.3:9) joined together, fitly framed according to the pattern of teaching, just as there is one Body comprising many members fitly framed together and blessed through and from the Head (Ephesians 4:16). Each component of the Temple is a necessary part of the one structure, becoming such through being built in, to become an integral part of the divine structure of collective testimony (Ephesians 2:21,22). As Paul could say, "in whom (i.e. the Lord) ye also are builded together ..." referring of course, to those in Ephesus linked with Corinth and other churches of God, forming the habitation of God in the Spirit.

1 Peter 2

Writing to those in churches of God in the five provinces in the northern and western areas of Asia Minor, the apostle Peter reminds them of their former vain manner of life until they came to Christ as repentant sinners and believed the Word of good tidings preached (1:25). Now, in churches of God, they "come" (continue coming) not as sinners for salvation which is once-for-all, but in collective approach as a worshipping and serving people. They draw near (v.4), offer up (v.5) and show forth (v.9). In doing this continually they reap rich blessing. This is on-going service of the people of God.

Peter has in mind the constructional materials of a building and uses the imagery of stones to convey the spiritual truth of God's desire for united service according to a prescribed pattern. They are built up a spiritual house (v.5), living stones joined to THE LIVING STONE, brought together and moulded together, not rough and unfinished stones haphazardly placed, but set in order in keeping with the divine plan. They were not freelance individualists going where they liked and doing what they liked. Conscious of the setting apart by the Spirit to obedience (1:2) through the work of sanctification individually and collectively (Hebrews 13:12), they sought to give expression to their state as a house, a priesthood, a race, a nation and a people. Thus the Spirit of God dwelt, worked and blessed in those days, and can do, and does today among those who conform to the apostles, and prophets teaching of Christ as Lord. Sadly, men reject the Saviour still to their eternal peril; believers can reject the Chief Comer Stone of spiritual Zion (1 Peter 2:6) to their loss. May we own Him as Lord and Saviour, Jesus Christ.

CHAPTER EIGHT: NEW TESTAMENT EMBLEMS OF THE HOLY SPIRIT (MICHAEL ELLIOTT)

A Dove

The word of the Lord to Isaiah speaks prophetically of the Christ to come: "Behold My Servant, whom I uphold ... I have put My Spirit upon Him" (Isaiah 42:1). This was demonstrated immediately after the Lord Jesus was baptized by John: "the heaven was opened, and the Holy Spirit descended in a bodily form, as a dove, upon Him" (Luke 3:21,22).

It is clear from this verse and from John's own witness (John 1:32) that this was a literal and not a poetic description. This was God's proof to him that Jesus was the Christ: "And I have seen, and have borne witness that this is the Son of God" (John 1:34). There must be something vital for us in this episode, not only of the Lord's example of baptism, but also of the manifestation of the Holy Spirit in such a way. Certainly it is a remarkable fulfilment of the Isaiah scripture and is the first emblem adopted by the Spirit in the New Testament.

The appearing of the Spirit in the bodily form of a dove cannot be separated from the incident on the bank of the Jordan. The Lord's baptism points the way of obedience by faith to those who would follow, and signifies also His coming baptism into death. God, His Father, has seen all and is well pleased with His beloved

Son, and the Holy Spirit graciously descends upon Him in public testimony of heaven's approval of this Man.

The dove is emblematic of the unity and harmony of the Triune God as the Lord Jesus, the perfect Man, begins His life work. Here was a Man who was holy, who would not fail to please God and on whom the Holy Spirit could descend and remain. It was from an open heaven that the Dove-Spirit came down and rested upon Him.

How different from that occasion when the first dove was sent out of the ark to search for land, but "found no rest for the sole of her foot" (Genesis 8:9). The coming into the world of the Son of God now made it possible for the Spirit of God to find a place to rest in a Man of flesh and blood, but without sin.

The dove is also widely used as a symbol of peace and gentleness. These are characteristics of the Lord. Not only did He bring peace to others, He was at peace within Himself. True, He was a Man of sorrows; true, He agonized in the Garden, and finally He was forsaken by His God on the Cross. He possessed, nevertheless, a perfect character with no dark place of self-doubt or inner fear in His heart. Indeed the heart of Christ is beautiful in its dovelike gentleness (Matthew 11:29). The Holy Spirit filled Him in all that He did, but never again was He revealed as the Dove-Spirit as on that momentous day by the Jordan. For the Spirit will take whatever form, within the will of God, suits His marvellous purposes.

Wind

Nicodemus, the Pharisee, was grappling with the new teaching of Jesus. The Holy Spirit was touching him mysteriously as the Lord explained: "The wind bloweth where it listeth, and thou hearest the voice thereof but knowest not whence it cometh, and whither it goeth" (John 3:8). Nothing of this could be seen. It was not a natural phenomenon. This aspect of the Spirit's work is often the most amazing, for He deals with each soul personally and secretly. As the unseen wind blows, so the Spirit draws souls to Christ, and a spiritual creature is born from above. Nicodemus felt the soft but compelling breeze of the Spirit on his soul. He believed, either that night or subsequently, and appreciated what the Saviour meant by, "That which is born of the flesh is flesh; and that which is born of the Spirit is spirit" (John 3:6).

The wind-emblem recurs in Acts 2, but in a most dramatic fashion. The disciples were gathered together on the day of Pentecost, the Lord having ascended into heaven, and were waiting, when: "Suddenly there came from heaven a sound as of the rushing of a mighty wind ... and there appeared unto them tongues parting asunder, like as of fire; and it sat upon each one of them" (Acts 2:2-4).

Here the inrushing Spirit is audible and visible. A mighty wind and tongues parting asunder were signs not only of His Presence, but also of the Spirit's first indwelling of believers on Christ. The Lord's words in Mark are fulfilled: "There be some here of them that stand by, which shall in no wise taste of death, till they see the kingdom of God come with power" (Mark 9:1).

As the Lord had promised shortly before His 'ascension (Luke 24:49), power would characterize the Spirit's coming upon them. They saw it and received it, the power of the indwelling Spirit. Filled with power they spoke the Name of the Lord without fear in other tongues as led by the Spirit. These happenings were unique to the apostles, eyewitnesses of the sufferings of Christ and the first to receive the Holy Spirit The mighty wind and tongues parting asunder unmistakably demonstrated that something revolutionary was occurring, and God was setting them apart as chosen vessels. Power was given to heal, to prophesy and to speak in other tongues, all apostolic gifts for their day.

Fire

As a result they were on fire with spiritual energy from the Lord: and as in the incident of the burning bush, they were not consumed by the fire. The Person of the Holy Spirit was indwelling them, giving them power and a burning heart, but their own personalities remained intact. Today His power and fire are still given to those who will receive Him.

Water

Our last emblem depicts the Holy Spirit by means of one of the most basic elements of life - water: If any man thirst, let him come unto Me, and drink. He that believeth on Me, as the scripture hath said, out of his belly shall flow rivers of living water. But this spake He of the Spirit, which they that believed on Him were to receive" (John 7:37-39). What a wonderful picture the Lord paints of the Spirit's capacity to quench spiritually the parched souls of men and women enabling Christlikeness to flow out towards others! The living water emblem reveals the Holy Spirit not given sparingly (John 3:34), but to overflowing.

Tremendous! Through simple faith in Christ, the whole reservoir of God's blessing is at the child of God's disposal and the only limiting factor is the willingness to drink. How sad if the river of living water should become a trickle, or a pool without inlet or outlet. Let us drink deeply through communion with the Lord in prayer and through His Word, and the outflowing of the Spirit will be seen in our living.

The Holy Spirit does not adopt these emblems idly. They portray His majesty and power and yet His gentleness in dealing with sinful man. We have seen Him in wind, fire and water and as a dove, each one revealing a facet of His Person. Yet none of them can adequately define Him, for He is God the Spirit, beyond our comprehension. He, the Holy Spirit, on the other hand knows us and loves us, as He also knows the heart of God and in everything acts to His greater glory. "Even so the things of God none knoweth, save the Spirit of God" (1 Corinthians 2:11).

CHAPTER NINE: NAMES AND TITLES OF THE HOLY SPIRIT (KEN DRAIN)

When studying the names and titles of the Holy Spirit one cannot but be impressed by the intimate inter-relationship between God the Father, God the Son and God the Holy Spirit. To fail to grasp the reality to the Trinity would inevitably render our study of little value. To recognize clearly the truth of the Trinity will, however, enable us to gain great benefit from the subject. The title most commonly used today, the Holy Spirit, highlights from the beginning that the Spirit is one in absolute holiness and purity with God, the "Holy Father" (John 17:11), and the Son, of whom the angel Gabriel said, "that which is to be born shall be called holy, the Son of God" (Luke 1:35).

It may focus our attention if we consider our subject under four main headings: (1) Divine Association, (2) Intellect, (3) Character, (4) Outworking.

1. Divine Association

By far the greatest number of references to the Holy Spirit are in the term Spirit of God, from the second verse in the Bible, where we read of the Spirit of God moving upon the face of the waters, right through to the last chapter of Revelation, when the Spirit and the bride say, Come (Revelation 22:17). Immediately we are introduced to one of the fundamentals of Holy Scripture. The Holy Spirit is fully divine. As a child I used to think in reference to the Trinity that the Father was the senior element, the Son was the one with whom we identified and the Spirit was a somewhat intangible element in the background. More maturely, one learns just how fully the Holy Spirit is involved in our lives.

Elizabeth was filled with the Holy Spirit when Mary the mother of Jesus came to visit, and spoke such beautiful words about the coming Lord (Luke 1:42). Elizabeth's husband Zacharias was filled with the Holy Spirit when he prophesied the future role of his son John (Luke 1:67). Peter was filled with the Holy Spirit as he addressed the religious leaders in Jerusalem and caused his hearers to marvel. Saul was filled with the Holy Spirit when he regained his sight (Acts 9:17), and again as Paul, when Elymas lost his sight (Acts 13:9).

So today, when we crucify to ourselves the world and mortify the flesh, we may be filled with the Spirit of God. When talking a drink of clear pure water we would not use a vessel which had the remains of cold coffee in it, but would wash out thoroughly the residue and only use a clean vessel. What a gracious thought that the Saviour will use us as vessels in His service and fill us with His Spirit!

As if to reinforce the divine nature of the Holy Spirit Isaiah tells us in chapter 61 verse 1 of the Spirit of the Lord God and indeed the Saviour Himself quoted this expression in the synagogue when He read from the book of Isaiah. In that wonderful epistle of Paul to the Church at Corinth he describes the transformation of believer from glory to glory into the image of the Lord Jesus through the Lord the Spirit (2 Corinthians 3:18). Reinforcing this association Peter tells us that the Spirit of God is also the Spirit of glory (1 Peter 4:14). How sacred it is to know that the Spirit of the Lord God enables us to reflect the glory of Christ Paul brings the whole concept very much alive by reminding the saints that He is the Spirit of the Living God. This is no lifeless doctrine, but teaching which is living and active, presenting the Divine Spirit as the source of spiritual vitality.

The Holy Spirit's intrinsic association with the Son is shown when Paul tells the disciples in Rome that the Spirit who indwells them is the Spirit of Christ (Romans 8:9). What closer relationship need we seek than to know that the Comforter who was sent to us is indeed the very Spirit of Christ, inextricably linking us to our Saviour, who although not present with us in bodily form indwells our very being through His Spirit. It was that selfsame Spirit who was in the prophets long before the birth of Christ (1 Peter 1:11).

2. Intellect

We read of numerous attributes to the intellect of the Holy Spirit, the Spirit of knowledge, the Spirit of understanding, the Spirit of wisdom. God does not demand the intellect of this world to give impression to His will. The man of high academic achievement and the man of modest learning may both be used mightily by God because they may both be filled with His knowledge, His understanding, His wisdom, and these are on an entirely different plane of intellect. Gods ways are not our ways neither are His thoughts our thoughts.

What closer relationship need we seek, than to know that the Comforter who was sent to us is indeed the very Spirit of Christ, inextricably linking us to our Saviour, who although not present with us in bodily form indwells our very being through His Spirit.

So let us study God's Word and His ways and open our minds to the refreshing education of the Holy Spirit. So often our decisions and interpretations are man led rather than Spirit led. How humble was the confession of that great King Solomon, when he told God that he was but a little child and asked for an understanding heart. God gave him wisdom and understanding to the extent that his wisdom excelled the wisdom of all the children of the east, and all the wisdom of Egypt (1 Kings 4:29,30). Divine wisdom is available to us through the Spirit of wisdom.

3. Character

It is quite clear that the characteristics of the Holy Spirit must be identical to those of the Son of God. How often we read of the grace of the Lord Jesus Christ. And so it comes as no surprise to read prophetically in Zechariah 12:10 of the Spirit of grace. Yet what a note of warning is contained in Hebrews 10:29: "Of how much sorer punishment, think ye, shall he be judged worthy, who hath ... done despite unto the Spirit of grace?"

John, in his Gospel closely relates grace with truth as two characteristics foreign to fallen man but brought back again through the Lord Jesus Christ "grace and truth came by Jesus Christ" (John 1:17). How fitting therefore that the Spirit of grace is also the Spirit of truth so often referred to by John. The outworking of grace and truth in the believer are closely related to the indwelling of the Holy Spirit. The Lord gave us the Spirit of truth to be with us for ever (John 14:16,17).

4. Outworking

The outworking of the Holy Spirit in our lives is manifold and quite clearly would warrant extensive further study. He is the Comforter, the Spirit of counsel, promise and prophecy. When the Lord was on earth He was able to console, comfort and draw near to the people. When He returned to His Father He left with us "the Comforter" or the Holy Spirit, and how dependant on this source of comfort we are today. Never will He leave us comfortless or that would mean that the Spirit has been taken out of our lives.

No legal document could more definitely ratify the believer's position in Christ than the seal which is put on our salvation by the Holy Spirit of promise. Our eternal inheritance is sure and steadfast, as a gift graciously bestowed from God and not negotiated by mutual agreement.

Having briefly touched on a number of the names and titles of the Holy Spirit, I do trust that we all may see Him as a close and intimate Person who leads and directs us into a richer and fuller appreciation of our Saviour.

CHAPTER TEN: A SECOND BLESSING OF THE HOLY SPIRIT? (GEORGE PRASHER)

With the tide of the "new Pentecostalism" now flowing strongly, and often sensationally, among some of the "historic denominations", it is instructive to analyse certain major teachings which are fundamental to the spiritual outlook of all these movements. One feature is their insistence upon a certain pattern of spiritual crisis in the experience of every child of God.

Stated in general terms, this teaching requires that after the new birth there is a separate and fuller experience of visitation by the Holy Spirit. This experience is represented as the most important step in a believer's life after he knows he has been born again. It is something to be given the highest priority. He must wait and pray and concentrate his whole desire upon it. He should never be satisfied until he has attained to this definite crisis in which he has proof to his natural senses of a special visitation. Different labels are attached to these experiences by different exponents of the Pentecostal outlook, but all are based on this common pattern of working towards a crisis of spiritual manifestation.

Does God's word in fact teach the believer to expect and strive for such an experience as the most important step in his spiritual life after he has put saving faith in the Lord Jesus? Let us consider what the Scriptures reveal of the believer's experience of the Holy Spirit from the day of Pentecost onwards. Few will dispute that truth applicable to the believer in the present time is exemplified in the Acts and expounded in the Epistles. That is to say, every major doctrine of the Lord which is binding on disciples throughout this dispensation will be fully substantiated in that portion of God's word from Acts chapter 1 to the end of Jude. This in no way detracts from the equal inspiration of all Scripture, but simply emphasizes to the present-day disciple the importance of truth particularly apposite to the age in which he lives. With this in mind, let us consider what God has to say about the believer and the Holy Spirit in the Acts and the Epistles.

Not once are we told to expect or to pray for this special experience!

This may be confirmed by every enquirer who cares to read again through the books in question. Then does it not seem extraordinary to urge every believer towards a crisis of experience with the Holy Spirit as the only door to fullness of spiritual life and power?

In marked contrast to this school of teaching which advocates a "crisis pattern" of Holy Spirit manifestation for every believer, the Epistles set before us a pattern of spiritual growth. Truths governing the believer's experience of the Holy Spirit are clearly stated. The Holy Spirit is sent by the Father into the heart of the believer at the moment he puts faith in Christ as Saviour (see Galatians 4.6, which links the believer's relationship as a child of God with the receiving of the Holy Spirit). At that time the believer is baptized in the Holy Spirit, for he cannot be a member of the Church the Body except the Lord Jesus baptize him in the Holy Spirit into the Body (1 Corinthians 12:13). From that time the Holy Spirit indwells him (1 Corinthians 6:19).

The doctrine of the Epistles regarding the Holy Spirit in the believer consistently assumes that each believer has received the Holy Spirit, has been baptized in the Holy Spirit, has been sealed with the Holy Spirit. Yet these Epistles exhort towards a constant exercise in knowing the fullness of the Holy Spirit (Ephesians 5:18), walking by the Spirit (Galatians 5:25), taking care neither to grieve nor quench the Spirit (Ephesians 4:30; 1 Thessalonians 5:19). This is growth through daily experience, a growth which may be maintained only by unremitting faith in and obedience to the word of God.

In confirmation of this, let us hear again the outpourings of the apostle Paul's great heart desires for the disciples of his day. The Holy Spirit has recorded several of these prayers for our instruction. Not once did Paul pray for such a crisis of spiritual manifestation as we are now told should be, the supreme quest of all believers. The burden of his prayers was for their spiritual growth, based upon the settled reality of the indwelling Spirit of God (see Ephesians 1:16-23, 3:14-19; Philippians 1:8-11; Colossians 1:9-11, 2:1-3).

Similarly, were this crisis experience the mind of God, we should expect the need to strive for it to be prominent in the exhortations of the Epistles. Why then do we look for this in vain? We can only conclude that an entirely wrong emphasis is given by all who advocate such teachings. This conclusion is strengthened when we hear the contradictory doctrinal explanations offered by those claiming to have attained these experiences. It will be useful to examine four of these:

A) The Crisis Experience claimed as Assurance of Salvation. There are those who claim that until one has had a spiritual manifestation marked by speaking in tongues, there is no assurance that one is truly a saved person. This extreme heresy is quoted to illustrate the lengths to which a wrong premise has led some earnest seekers after a crisis of "manifestation in the realm of the Spirit".

B) The Crisis Experience claimed as "The Baptism of the Holy Spirit". Those who advocate this view follow the line that the disciples were born again through faith in Christ as recorded in the Gospels, but were taught to pray for the Holy Spirit (Luke 11.13), and, after waiting in prayer as recorded in Acts 1, they were baptized in the Holy Spirit on the Day of Pentecost. This sequence in the experience of those who companied with the Lord is wrongly applied to the present-day believer, who is urged to strive in prayer until he is vouchsafed a supernatural manifestation of the "baptism of the Holy Spirit".

Now this mode of argument is deceptive. It ignores the historical setting of the apostles' experience. For they lived in a period of transition from the dispensation of law to the dispensation of grace. What occurred in their experience was unique to believers of the generation who had believed in the Lord Jesus before the day of Pentecost. For the first time in human history they were baptized in the Holy Spirit on that day. Before that time they knew the Holy Spirit's presence with them, but the Lord had taught them to look forward to something more: "He abideth with you, and shall be in you" (John 14.16,17). Shortly before His ascension to the Father, He confirmed, "Ye shall be baptized in the Holy Spirit not many days hence" (Acts 1:5). It is therefore misleading to build a doctrine for believers of this age upon the experiences of apostles whose knowledge of the Lord began before the start of the present dispensation.

Actually there are only seven references to baptism in the Holy Spirit in the New Testament (note that "Baptism of the Spirit" is not a scriptural term.) Six of these references have to do with the Lord's outpouring of the Holy Spirit at Pentecost. The Lord Himself would be the Baptizer. He would baptize believers in the Holy Spirit; that is, the Holy Spirit would be the element in which they would be baptized by Him. The seventh occurrence is in 1 Corinthians 12.13: "For in one Spirit were we all baptized into one body, whether Jews or Greeks, whether bond or free; and were all made to drink of one Spirit."

Prayerful reflection on this verse will bring much light. For it states absolutely that to be one with Christ as a member of His Body, a person must be baptized in the Holy Spirit. That the Lord Jesus is the Baptizer is clear from four of the six references given above. So that every believer is, at the time of the new birth, baptized by the Lord Jesus in the Holy Spirit into the Body of Christ. This mystery must be accepted by faith. It accords perfectly with Peter's words in Acts 11.17: "If then God gave unto them the like gift as He did also unto us, when we believed on the Lord Jesus Christ, who was I, that I could withstand God?"

The Holy Spirit is a gift from God, bestowed on every believer when baptized in the Spirit at the time of the new birth. The gift is bestowed purely on the principle of faith -see, for example, John 7:39; Acts 10:43-48; Galatians 3:2,14; Ephesians 1:13.

Some have difficulty regarding the two cases recorded in Acts chapters 8 and 19. In chapter 8, the Samaritans did not receive the Holy Spirit until Peter and John came from Jerusalem and laid their hands on them, although they had accepted the Saviour under Philip's ministry, and had been baptized in the Name of the Lord Jesus. Again, Paul discovered certain disciples at Ephesus who had been taught only the baptism of John; the Holy Spirit came upon them and they spoke in tongues when Paul laid his hands on them, after their reception of the gospel and their baptism in the Name of the Lord Jesus There were special reasons for these exceptional cases. In the first case, we need only recall the deep cleavage which had traditionally obtained between Jews and Samaritans (John 4.9). Lest that division should be perpetuated in the early churches of God, the gift of the Holy Spirit was withheld until the apostles came from Jerusalem, thus welding the Samaritan work in close unity with that in Judea. In the second, the manifestation of tongues when these disciples of John accepted the gospel would emphasize to them the distinctive character of the truth they had now embraced.

It would be unsound to build up a doctrine on such exceptional cases. Basic doctrine on any subject must be built on the main body of teaching in the Scriptures. Exceptions serve to emphasize a general rule rather than contradict it. What then do we find was the general rule regarding baptism in the Holy Spirit? The case of Cornelius and his friends, in Acts chapter 10, illustrates the normal experience of the Gentile believers in this age- as they received the word, the Holy Spirit fell on them. They were born again, and simultaneously baptized in one Spirit into the Body of Christ. In their case this baptism was marked with outward manifestations, to teach Peter and his Jewish brethren that "God had also to the Gentiles granted repentance unto life" (Acts 11:18). From that time forward, the many who accepted the gospel were all baptized in one Spirit into one Body upon putting faith in the Lord Jesus (compare, for example, Acts 18:11 and 1 Corinthians 12:13).

The outpouring of the Spirit at Pentecost, and the three cases quoted from Acts 8, 10, and 19, all confirm how effortless was this reception of the gift of the Holy Spirit. There was no striving or crying for the gift. Nor was it dependent upon the holiness of life of those who received it. Every believer received the Spirit as a gift from God, and was baptized in one Spirit into the Body of Christ. This was as much part of his heritage through faith in the Lord Jesus as the gift of everlasting life or the forgiveness of sins.

C) The Crisis Experience claimed as confirmed by Tongues. Some teachers extend the foregoing view by asserting that the crisis of the "Baptism of the Holy Spirit" is not truly experienced unless one has spoken in tongues. This is quite out of line with scriptural precedent. There are only three places in the whole story of the Acts where speaking in tongues is mentioned – 2:4, 10:46, and 19:6. The three thousand saved on the day of Pentecost were all baptized in one Spirit into one Body; so were the additional converts of Acts 4; also the eunuch of Acts 8, and the apostle Paul in Acts 9; to say nothing of the multitudes of converts reached during the missionary journeys of Paul and others. Yet in none of these cases does the Spirit record any miraculous manifestation accompanying the great reality of baptism in the Holy Spirit. We rightly conclude that in the great majority of cases baptism in the Spirit into the Body of Christ took place without any outward proof to the natural senses. So it has been with multitudes of believers down to the present day. Every born-again one, being a member of the Body of Christ, must necessarily have been baptized in the Holy Spirit.

This is confirmed by comparing the great "proof text" of 1 Corinthians 12:13 with verse 30 of that chapter. Verse 30 implies that all had not spoken with tongues; yet all had been baptized in the Holy Spirit.

D) The Crisis Experience claimed as proof of the Holy Spirit's Fullness. There are other Pentecostals who teach that, whereas the believer is baptized in the Holy Spirit at the moment of the new birth, he must nevertheless seek for a further special blessing, which is the only true evidence of attaining the fullness of the Holy Spirit. In effect, what many describe as a "baptism of the Holy Spirit" others describe as "a filling with the Spirit". It is still presented as a marked crisis towards which every believer must strive until he attains it. It will be an unmistakable experience, obvious to the natural senses, even though the manifestation may vary in detail from person to person.

This change of terminology from "baptism of the Spirit" to "fullness of the Spirit" is scripturally untenable. For we are exhorted to be "filled with the Spirit" (Ephesians 5.18) as a matter of habitual exercise, not of unique crisis. We have examples of men whose spiritual character was such that they could be described as "full of the Holy Spirit", that is, habitually so (see Acts 6:5, 11:24).

Hungering and Thirsting That We May Be Filled

The special object of this chapter is to show that God's Word does not lead the believer to expect that by a sudden crisis in his spiritual life he will automatically be raised to a higher plane of Christian experience. The essential conditions for spiritual growth must be maintained if life-long progress is to be known. There will be a proper hungering and thirsting after a fuller knowledge of Christ and a greater resulting power in service. One example of such longings is expressed for us in Paul's prayer for the Ephesians:

> "That ye may be strengthened with power through His Spirit in the inward man; that Christ may dwell in your hearts through faith; to the end that ye, being rooted and grounded in love, may be strong to apprehend with all the saints what is the breadth and length and height and depth, and to know the love of Christ which passeth knowledge, that ye may be filled unto all the fullness of God" (Ephesians 3:16-19).

If yearnings for a deeper and fuller knowledge of God are not stirred in the believer's heart by the Holy Spirit there is something lacking in his experience. Care is needed lest earnest exercise for a continuing fullness of the Holy Spirit be neglected. Nor must we overlook that some Christians who have never claimed spiritual manifestations have nevertheless known crises in their spiritual life which have left indelible impressions. Many have borne witness to God's dealings with them in this way. Deep exercise for greater holiness of life or power in witness have been followed by an unforgettable realization of the presence of God, and a fullness of the Holy Spirit which has marked a distinct transformation of their spiritual life. To God be the glory for such experiences and their results!

Yet we must guard against building wrong doctrine on these experiences. The instructed believer appreciates that God in His sovereignty grants these experiences to some; but He has not guaranteed them to all. There is a useful parallel in God's dealings with Israel in Old Testament times. All earnest Israelites could attain a measure of spiritual growth and enlightenment simply by ensuring that the basic condition of heart was right. "What doth the LORD require of thee, but to do justly, and to love mercy, and to walk humbly with thy God?" Through some, however, God had a special purpose, land in fitting them for their tasks He manifested Himself uniquely to them. He spoke "in divers portions and in divers manners". Moses stood with unshod feet as the Voice of the eternal God spoke to him from the burning bush; Elijah covered his face with his mantle at the cave entrance as the still small voice filled his heart with awe; Isaiah saw the Lord high and lifted up; Daniel's comeliness was turned to corruption at the divine presence. If then a believer should be vouchsafed some particular experience of God's manifest presence, let him cherish the blessing which he has received through it; but it may not be God's will for another to have an identical experience.

> "But ye, beloved, building up yourselves on your most holy faith, praying in the Holy Spirit, keep yourselves in the love of God, looking for the mercy of our Lord Jesus Christ unto eternal life" (Jude 20-21).

CHAPTER ELEVEN: THE HOLY SPIRIT INDWELLING THE BELIEVER (JOHN KERR)

After initially convicting us of our sinner need before God and bringing us to repentance, the Holy Spirit witnesses with our spirits that we are children of God (Romans 8:16). The quickening that took place at the new birth was dependent on our response to the Holy Spirit's voice in the gospel message, through which message we were saved (1 Corinthians 15:2). Following on from this, we would naturally expect that just as we cannot be reconciled to God apart from responding to the Holy Spirit, so we cannot live victorious Christian lives apart from an on-going response to that self-same Spirit Furthermore, how better to make Him available to us than to place Him within us at the new birth. Then He becomes our permanent Guest and the duty of every believer is to respond to His leading. "Those who are led by the Spirit of God are sons of God" (Romans 8:14); in other words the way to identify true likeness to God is to recognize the Spirit's leading in a believer's life.

The purpose of this chapter then is twofold, firstly to establish that the Holy Spirit does in fact permanently indwell each believer and thereafter to discuss how best the believer can respond to His leading. These two points are presented as propositions, putting them to the test by the application of relevant scriptures.

ProposItion 1

The Holy Spirit permanently indwells each believer from the moment of the new birth. When our Saviour said of the Holy Spirit that He would abide with the disciples for ever, dwell with them and be in them (John 14:16-17) what did He mean? In contrast to this world which neither sees the Holy Spirit nor knows Him, the disciples were reminded that He already was with them, for they knew Him and indeed had no doubt felt His power when they had gone forth two by two to work miracles (Luke 10:1-9). However, they were now to be prepared for the fuller gift of the Holy Spirit at Pentecost and the distinct change introduced by that new experience, namely that the Holy Spirit was going to be "in them" and "with them for ever".

All of this was clearly predicted by the Lord. This permanent abiding was in contrast to the separation which was about to take place when the Lord departed, for He would come again in the Person of the Holy Spirit and this time there would be no parting. The New Testament letters reinforce this new role of the Holy Spirit when, for example, Paul states in 1 Corinthians 6 verse 19 that the believer's physical body is a temple of the Holy Spirit.

This "flesh and bones container" is clearly a dwelling place of the Holy Spirit. It is not surprising, therefore, that the apostle adds "glorify God in your body". God indwelling the believer in the Person of the Holy Spirit is set out in 1 John chapter 4 where we read "greater is He that is in you than he that is in the world". God is in us "because He has given us of His Spirit" (v.13) and "whosoever shall confess that Jesus is the Son of God, God abideth in Him" (v.15).

From Ephesians chapter 1 verse 13 we learn that having believed we were sealed with (not by) the Holy Spirit, a guarantee against the future, which guarantee is with us as a pledge until the day of redemption, the day when our redemption is complete, when soul and body will be reunited at the rapture (Ephesians 4:30). As far as the earthly life and earthly body of the believer are concerned, the Holy Spirit will have done His work, coming to us at the new birth, taking up residence in our bodies and abiding with us for life's journey.

Another expression in the New Testament which is used of the Holy Spirit in relation to the believer is the word anointing. Prophets, priests and kings were all anointed (i.e. set apart for a particular service). The anointing was indicated by pouring oil on the head and since oil is a symbol for the Holy Spirit it is not surprising to find the Holy Spirit linked with anointing in the New Testament. It would appear from Acts 10 verses 43 to 45 and 2 Corinthians 1 verses 21 and 22 that the giving of the Holy Spirit to the believer at conversion is an anointing by God, 1 John chapter 2 verses 20 and 27 associate the anointing with that aspect of the Holy Spirit's work which teaches us truth and reveals Christ. Of course we must abide in Christ for that teaching to be wholly effective.

Indwelt, sealed, anointed; these are all consistent with the fact that the believer, saved at the new birth from the eternal punishment his sins deserve, cannot lose that salvation.

Proposition 2

There is a clear responsibility resting on the believer to respond daily to the leading of the indwelling Spirit. If this leading is not recognized or, if recognized, the response is inadequate a great purpose of the Christian life will be missed. Since the Holy Spirit is a gift common to all believers it should be clear that the matter we now address is not only for leaders and eminent saints, but for all children of God.

Let us come again to Romans chapter 8 verse 14 which reads "as many as are led by the Spirit of God, these are sons of God". Now the clear purpose of this leading is to infuse into us the character of Christ (see 2 Corinthians 3:18). The intention is to produce holiness and enable sin to be conquered not to escape trials of suffering, but to overcome. The Holy Spirit should become the regulative influence in our lives, controlling all our actions. It is not being carried, for that is not being led, neither is one led when one goes one's own way, for to lead is to take control, and this we must allow the Holy Spirit to do.

It has been said that when we are led we are always conscious of the road on which we travel - its roughness, steepness, twists and turns. The Holy Spirit has put us on the right path, now He plans to keep us there. It is not enough to be "in Christ", it is not enough to be "in the Lord", we must walk by the Spirit (Galatians 5:16). Under the control of the Spirit we discipline our natural selves and, in certain cases, reduce them to a condition of death resulting in spiritual life in the Spirit (Romans 8:13). The fulness of this is referred to by the Lord in John chapter 7 verses 38 and 39. These come from the indwelling Holy Spirit and flow out to others. Our joy in the Lord will be full, and evident to all who meet us. "Sons of God" are so different from all others.

What a marvellous source of power is within us, for consider these scriptures - "Strengthened with power through His Spirit in the inward man" (Ephesians 3:16), "greater is He that is in you than he that is in the world" (1 John 4:4). Do you see triumphs in the lives of other Christians that you don't see in your own? You have the same Holy Spirit and the same power - only you must let Him lead. Don't press on with your own ideas and expect God to stop them, but follow His leading and God will infuse His power into you by the Holy Spirit. Only then can you be truly victorious.

A consideration of the indwelling Spirit would hardly be complete without a reference to the fruit of the Spirit (Galatians 5:22-23). As often pointed out, it is one fruit with nine characteristics. We do not select only what suits us or might appeal to our natural characteristics. We are meant to produce them all, thereby reproducing Christ's character within us. "Since we live by the Spirit, let us keep in step with the Spirit" (Galatians 5:25 NIV).

We see the Holy Spirit as our permanent guest, our powerful leader, our seal and our private comforter. He is with us, in us, leading, guiding, teaching and filling. All of this is indeed a treasure in an earthen vessel (2 Corinthians 4:7). In view of this, what manner of persons ought we to be in all holy living and godliness (2 Peter 3:11). "Speaking one to another in psalms and hymns and spiritual songs, singing and making melody with your heart to the Lord; giving thanks always for all things in the Name of our Lord Jesus Christ to God' even the Father; subjecting yourselves one to another in the fear of Christ (Ephesians 5:19-21).

CHAPTER TWELVE: THE CHARISMATIC GIFTS OF THE HOLY SPIRIT (GEORGE PRASHER)

What Were 'Gifts of the Holy Spirit'?

This question assumes special importance because of frequent modern reference to 'charismatic gifts', by which are meant such gifts as prophecies, healings, or speaking in tongues. It should be noted that scriptural usage does not distinguish such gifts as 'charismatic'. The Greek word *charisma* has the basic meaning of a gift involving grace or favour. It is indeed applied directly to gifts of healings (1 Corinthians 12:9), and by implication to tongues and prophecy (1 Corinthians 12:30; 13:2). But it is equally used in respect of the gift of eternal life (Romans 6:23) or of Israel's special favours under sovereign divine choice (Romans 11:29).

Scripturally, therefore, we must include in our consideration of gifts of the Holy Spirit not only the nine manifestations listed in 1 Corinthians 12:8-11, but such additional gifts as 'teachers, helps, governments' (1 Corinthians 12:28). Compare also Romans 12:6-8 and 1 Peter 4:10,11, where the Greek word translated 'gifts' is again *charisma*. The word translated 'gifts' in Hebrews 2:4 is not *charisma* but *merismos* (a dividing or distribution). As this refers to the confirmation of the Lord's word through the apostles by miraculous gifts, it is significant that *merismos* should be used. Scriptural guidance would therefore discourage the term 'charismatic gifts'. By referring to 'gifts of the Holy Spirit' or 'spiritual gifts' our thoughts will be more accurately related to Bible revelation.

Guidance from 1 Corinthians 12-14

In these three chapters God has enshrined for us His wise counsel regarding certain gifts of the Holy Spirit which were granted to disciples in the church of God in Corinth. This brief study is designed to review the setting in which those gifts found expression, and to place in scriptural perspective their purpose and usefulness. The subject matter of the three chapters may be summarised thus. Chapter Twelve discusses the gifts and their CO-ORDINATION. Chapter 13 describes loves as the MOTIVATION. Chapter 14 outlines the gifts and the resultant EDIFICATION.

The subject is not treated so fully in any other area of the New Testament: it is recommended that the three chapters be read through as a whole, for this helps towards a balanced understanding of the gifts of the Spirit in apostolic times. Principles established from these chapters have singular value in guiding our understanding of other New Testament references to spiritual gifts

The Gifts and Their Co-ordination (Chapter 12)

God's work, whether in natural creation or in redemptive purpose, is characterised by a diversity which He co-ordinates to effect His overall design. The work of the Triune God through disciples together forming the Church of God in Corinth was in harmony with this. The same Spirit, the same Lord, the same

God, effected diversities of gifts, ministrations and workings (1 Corinthians 12:4-6).

The greatest spiritual fulfillment for each individual disciple would be found within the setting designed by God for spiritual service - a church of God. An individual might be blessed with certain gifts of the Spirit, but he would not be given all the gifts. It was ordained that by distribution of the gifts among different disciples each would feel his dependence upon God's working through others also.

God's most effectual working would be by means of co-ordinating different manifestations of the Spirit through a variety of individuals, "to each one severally, even as He will" (1 Corinthians 12:11). Here is divine wisdom for our guidance: independence brings spiritual loss, interdependence spiritual fulfilment.

A key point is established in verse 13, where it is asserted that all the disciples were baptised in one Spirit into one Body, and all made to drink of one Spirit, whatever their racial or social status. So the fact was that all who believed the gospel were baptised by the Lord Jesus in the Holy Spirit to become members of the Church which is His Body (compare Matthew 3:11 and Acts 11:16,17).

It should be particularly noted that this obtained even though some did not have the gifts of healings, tongues or miracles (verses 29,30). Despite the varying distribution of gifts, each believer was joined with Christ the Head as a member of His Body (compare Ephesians 5:23,30). Hence the remarkable word 'so also is Christ' (12:12). The definite article is placed before the word

'Christ' in the Greek, literally reading, 'so also is the Christ'. It is as though the members of the Church which is His Body are seen so closely identified with Him the Head that he and they together are in this context referred to as 'the Christ'.

On the basis of this great truth Paul proceeded to illustrate the co-ordination of spiritual gifts by reference to the working together of members of the natural body (verses 14-26). Foot, hand, ear and eye are each 'of the body' and are intended to function in harmony with other members. God has set the members in the human body 'even as it pleased Him'. Each member has a special function and is needed, some of the seemingly feeble being most necessary. This lucid parallel was applied to disciples in the Church of God in Corinth.

"Ye are the Body of Christ, and severally members thereof" (verse 27). It was not that disciples in the Corinthian church comprised the whole Body of Christ. Every believer was included in that Body. Verse 27 literally reads "Ye are Body of Christ" (no definite article before the noun soma). Because they were individually members of the Body they should function together in character with that fact.

Through Christ the Head they were joined in organic spiritual union, therefore this truth should govern all their relationships in service together within a church of God. They came behind in no gift (1:7), but their individual gifts, divided to each one severally according to the will of the Spirit, were to be used 'to profit withal' (verse 7). The Spirit who divided to each one the appropriate gift(s) must be allowed to control the co-ordination of those gifts for mutual blessing.

Love as the Motivation (Chapter 13)

The 'more excellent way' shown in this chapter demonstrates that God is more concerned about the motive which prompts the use of a spiritual gift than about the gift itself. We are readily the victims of our own weaknesses, from which only the balancing grace of Christ can keep us. To some of the disciples in the Corinthian church their Spirit-given gifts had become a cause of self-esteem and rivalry.

The gifts were intended to find expression in love to God and to fellow-disciples. There was danger that the gift of tongues could become a means of self-display, and that ability to prophesy or to know divine mysteries could lead to spiritual pride. Without love as the motivation, apparently brilliant expressions of gift were valueless (verses 1-3).

Characteristics of true love before God and others are detailed in verses 4-7. This was doubtless with a view to correcting attitudes which had arisen among the Corinthians through their preoccupation with certain spiritual gifts.

> "Love envieth not; ... vaunteth not itself, is not puffed up, doth not behave itself unseemly ... is not provoked" (1 Corinthians 13:4,5).

Some were puffed up with knowledge, others proud of their gifts, and there was selfish assertiveness in exercising gifts whether others could be edified as a result or not. This we may glean from the moderating counsel of 1 Corinthians 14:23,27,30, counsel which had to be given to correct these wrong attitudes.

Further to emphasize the basic importance of love as the motivation in all exercise of the spiritual gifts, the apostle proceeded (verse 8) to show that love will abide eternally. Prophecies and knowledge shall be done away, and tongues shall cease. All inclination to pride because of spiritual gifts would shrivel up in the perspective of eternity.

For instance, when we know as we are known how limited any present degree of knowledge will seem to be! As for prophecy and tongues, they will have no further relevance. Yet love will abide eternally, and the disciple of Christ should above all else follow after love. Only as love is the motivation could spiritual gifts yield anything of abiding value.

The Gifts and Edification (Chapter 14)

It was the divine intention that believers should be grouped together to form a church of God in their locality. The Acts of the Apostles describes the development of such churches of God, first in Jerusalem and then in other places as the gospel was spread more widely. When writing to the Church of God in Corinth on the subject of spiritual gifts Paul was led to stress in chapter 14 the central importance of the gifts being used to edify the church.

The Greek word translated edify is 'oikodomeo', literally meaning 'to build a house', but used figuratively in the sense of promoting the spiritual growth and development of believers. So the Corinthians were exhorted, "Since ye are zealous of spiritual gifts, seek that ye may abound unto the edifying of the church" (verse 12). With this in view the apostle pointed out certain disadvantages of the gift of tongues, and the superior usefulness of prophesying.

One speaking in a tongue was speaking to God rather than to men (verse 2); in the spirit he could be speaking mysteries, but if others could not understand they would not be edified; he would be edifying only himself (verse 4). But "he that prophesieth speaketh unto men edification, and comfort, and consolation" (verse 3), which would edify the church (verse 4).

Similarly in prayer, though a brother bless with the spirit, the unlearned could not say the Amen if he had not understood what had been said: "Thou verily givest thanks well, but the other is not edified" (verse 17). So Paul himself felt that despite being able to speak with tongues more than them all, in the church he would rather speak five words with his understanding, that he might instruct others also, than ten thousand words in a tongue (verses 18,19).

Then there was the effect on the unlearned or unbelieving who might attend gatherings of the church. If all spoke with tongues, the unbeliever would say they were mad. But if God's word was spoken forth by prophecy the message would be understood, "so he will fall down on his face and worship God, declaring that God is among you indeed" (v.25).

In summarizing his advice to the Corinthian church (verses 26-33) the keynote of the apostle's advice is "Let all things be done unto edifying". Even if an interpreter was present, not more than three should speak in a tongue; and if there was no interpreter, "let him keep silence in the church; and let him speak to himself and to God". There was to be orderliness, self-control and consideration for one another (vv.29-33,40).

It would seem from verses 34-38 that some of the women in the Corinthian church had wished to exercise certain gifts publicly when the church was assembled. This was firmly forbidden by the Lord through Paul - we note that the affirmation of Paul's authority from the Lord in verse 37 is closely related to his instruction that women should keep silent in the church (verse 34). So this is not merely 'Paul's opinion', it is the Lord's commandment. It is helpful to compare the following statements:

"Let him keep silence in the church" (verse 28)

"Let the first keep silence" (verse 30)

"Let the women keep silence in the churches" (verse 34).

There can be no question as to what Paul meant in verses 28 and 30. Is not the meaning in verse 34 exactly the same? He was not referring to irreverent chattering among women, as some have suggested, but he was correcting the wrong desire of some women to lead the assembly publicly, whether in prayer, prophesying or with a tongue. We read elsewhere of Philip's daughters prophesying (Acts 21:9), but the instruction given through Paul in 1 Corinthians 14:34-37 indicates that the exercise of this gift would not be at public meetings of the church.

This section of the epistle closes with a wisely balanced statement – "Wherefore, my brethren, desire earnestly to prophesy, and forbid not to speak with tongues. But let all things be done decently and in order" (verses 39,40).

Among all the spiritual gifts with which the Holy Spirit had enriched the Corinthian church, speaking with tongues had assumed an undue prominence in their spiritual experience together. The apostle was guided to write correcting this tendency, and in doing so imparted much valuable information about the spiritual gifts - the secret of their co-ordination, the vital need of love as the motivation, their being used for the edification of the church. The value of this scriptural instruction in our contemporary spiritual background and experience may now be further considered.

Scriptural Precedent and Modern Experience

The Christian today may often meet those who claim to have experienced certain gifts of the Holy Spirit such as were manifested in the apostolic era. In this, as in all matters of our Christian life, we shall find our guide and safeguard in the written Word.

From careful attention to scriptural precedent and teaching there emerge certain lines of principle by which claims to spiritual gifts can be assessed. "To the law and to the testimony!" (Isaiah 8:20) should be our watchword. Nine gifts of the Spirit are named in 1 Corinthians 12:8-10: The word of wisdom, The word of knowledge, Faith, Gifts of healings, Workings of miracles, Prophecy, Discerning of spirits, Divers kinds of tongues, The interpretation of tongues.

Of these nine, some are classed as 'greater gifts' (12:31). The relative importance of any gift would depend upon its usefulness is relation to the continuing development of God's purpose throughout the present age of grace. This great purpose centred in the spread of the gospel, with the resulting growth of the Church which is the Body of Christ, and the gathering of disciples into churches of God.

At the beginning of the age it was necessary to confirm the word of the Lord through the apostles "by signs and wonders, and by manifold powers, and by gifts of the Holy Spirit" (Hebrews 2:4). Hence the importance at that juncture of such gifts as healings, miracles, tongues and their interpretation. Moreover, during that early phase of the dispensation the written Word of the New Testament was incomplete. God therefore imparted the knowledge of His will through the word of wisdom, the word of knowledge and prophecy.

Once the great new revelation through Christ and the apostles had been confirmed, and its truths enshrined in the written New Testament, several gifts of the Holy Spirit no longer had the same importance. For God had given ample evidence that the new revelation was of divine origin. To continue miraculous manifestations beyond the apostolic era would take away from the distinctiveness of that era. Nor were further revelations needed or intended. The written Word would be an all-sufficient guide (2 Timothy 3:17; Jude v.3; Revelation 22:18,19). Special attention should be given to the Lord's words in John 14:12:

> "He that believeth on Me, the works that I do shall he do also; and greater works than these shall he do; because I go unto the Father".

This cannot apply to miraculous gifts. For in what way did even the apostles do greater workers than the Lord Himself? Their works were not greater in the sense of being more wonderful! Certainly the modern claimant to miraculous power does nothing comparable to the work of Christ. The 'greater works' are not greater signs. The Master's words apply to the world-wide extension of the kingdom of God by the work of the apostles and others, in contrast to the limitation of the Lord's own work to "the lost sheep of the house of Israel" (Matthew 10:5,6; 15:24).

Other gifts of the Spirit would, however, be of permanent importance for the continuing development of God's purpose in the making of disciples and in their spiritual well-being in churches of God. Prophecy, the word of wisdom and the word of knowledge, would find abiding expression in relation to the written Word.

The Holy Spirit would gift some to prophesy in the sense of speaking forth the scriptural message in terms of "edification, and comfort, and consolation" (1 Corinthians 14:3). To some would be given the gifts of knowledge in the interpretation of the Word; to others the gift of wisdom in application of the Word to current problems.

Those with a gift of faith would be of abiding helpfulness in the encouragement and upbuilding of the disciples. The discerning of spirits would operate through the testing of 'doctrines of demons' by truths of the written Word.

Tongues and Their Interpretation

Comparison of 1 Corinthians 12:31 with 14:1 suggests that prophecy was one of the greater gifts. By contrast, tongues and their interpretation were among the lesser. They had assumed undue prominence among the Corinthian disciples. It is noteworthy that among many believers today a similar desire to speak in tongues has assumed very great importance, despite its being one of the lesser gifts. This is of itself instructive. It reflects an imbalance in spiritual attitudes which the Word of God will at once adjust.

Added to this is the frequent linking of speaking in tongues with progressive experience in relation to the Holy Spirit. For instance, some assert that a believer is not baptised in the Holy Spirit until he speaks in tongues. Others aver that speaking in tongues is a necessary accompaniment of the fullness of the Spirit. Yet others have even taught that one cannot be sure of the Spirit's indwelling unless there has been an experience of speaking in tongues.

Whatever the variations of these teachings, they have in common that they make speaking in tongues an evidence or sign of some special phase of the Spirit's dealings with the believer. One brief word of Scripture exposes the fallacy of such teachings:

> "Tongues are for a sign, not to them that believe, but
> to the unbelieving" (1 Corinthians 14:22).

This illuminating word from the Lord will deliver the believer from the notion that he must have spoken in tongues before being indwelt by, or baptised in, or filled with the Holy Spirit. Rather, he will rest on the assurances of God's word in such places as 1 Corinthians 6:19 (as to the indwelling) or 12:13 (as to baptism in the Spirit). As to the fullness of the Spirit it is clear that this was not necessarily accompanied by a manifestation of tongues.

Peter was among those filled with the Spirit on successive occasions - the day of Pentecost (Acts 2:4), before the Sanhedrin (4:8) and among his own company (4:31). Yet tongues are mentioned only in Acts 2. Moreover, the disciples in Ephesus were exhorted to be filled with the Spirit (Ephesians 5:18) as a matter of normal Christian experience, quite apart from miraculous manifestations.

Nor is there the slightest hint in the New Testament that a desire to speak in tongues should be the believer's main objective after he has accepted Christ. The artificial stimulation of excitement to promote this experience is entirely unscriptural. In each recorded instance when God granted certain to speak in tongues the gift was poured out on them without their expectation or request (Acts 2:4; 10:46; 19:6).

These brief scriptural considerations illustrate the unsoundness of much associated at the present time with claims to tongues or their interpretation. Such claims are often related to wrong doctrinal exposition of Scripture regarding the Holy Spirit and the believer.

Indeed some who are seriously in error as to the Person of Christ and His redemptive work also claim this gift. If those speaking in tongues have such widely diverse spiritual outlooks, to what truth could God be bearing witness by their common exercise of the gift? (compare Hebrews 2:4).

Gifts of Healings

Claimants to these gifts have also gained continuing prominence in recent times. They believe that such powers of healing as were exercised by the apostles and others in the first century have been renewed. The nature of this claim should be carefully noted. For there is no question that God may be pleased to grant healing beyond all medical expectation in answer to prayer, where this is His will. But this is a different matter from claiming to have apostolic gifts of healings. Again we must be guided alone by Scripture.

A study of the Gospels and the Acts reveals certain general principles which governed the exercise of healing power, and these are helpful in considering modern claims to such gifts.

(1) The Principle of Discernment in the Healer

With the power to heal in the Name of the Lord Jesus went the ability to discern when it was the will of God to heal in any particular case. This was an essential feature of the gift as exercised by the apostles. For it was a guarantee that the precious Name of God's Son would not be dishonoured by attempted healings which failed.

This discernment is illustrated in Acts 3:4 and 14:9: both Peter and Paul looked intently on those they were about to heal, and in the case of the cripple at Lystra it is explained that Paul saw he had faith to be made whole. The fact that Paul left Trophimus sick at Miletus (2 Timothy 4:20) reflects the same truth of discernment in the healer. For Paul had the gift of healing, but on that occasion he must have discerned that it was not God's will for Trophimus to be healed immediately.

(2) The Principle of Unfailing and Absolute Restoration.

"This perfect soundness in the presence of you all" (Acts 3:16). The Holy Spirit's description through Luke of the perfect healing of this lame man may be taken as the true hallmark of all healing which resulted from the exercise of these gifts. It was a perfect healing, evident to all. One who had been well known as a life-long cripple was walking, leaping and praising God; and the following day he was still perfectly healed! (Acts 4:16).

Other examples include the palsied man of Lydda (9:34), the cripple of Lystra (14:10), the victim of fever and dysentery in Melita (28:8). In each case the disease was clearly defined, evident to all, and instantaneously and fully cured.

(3) The Principle of Divine Sovereignty.

The man at the Beautiful Gate of the Temple asked for alms and received miraculous healing. This was gratuitously bestowed by God in sovereign grace, just as the Lord cured the sick man at the Pool of Bethesda (John 5). There were often earnest seeking and ardent faith on the part of those healed, but these two illustrations show that it was not necessarily so. Faith was indispensable on the part of the healer; some who expressed little faith, if any, were cured.

(4) The Principle of the Modest Exercise of the Gift

The Lord frequently charged those He healed that they should not publicise what He had done for them (Matthew 9:30; Mark 5:43; 7:36; 8:26; Luke 5:14). Nor did the apostles use miracles as a means of publicity. The gift was exercised when the Holy Spirit made plain to His servants that God would be glorified by a miraculous expression of healing power. A danger is illustrated in Acts 3:12 and 14:11. Attention was all too readily focused on the human instruments of healing grace rather than on the deeper spiritual purpose of confirming divine truth.

When tested by these four principles, many modern claims to the recovery of New Testament gifts of healings are found wanting. It would be quite unmistakable if God were to grant a recurrence of such miracles as are seen in Scripture. Much that is claimed today is not comparable, either as to the type of affliction involved, or as to the character of the healing.

This is not to say that no benefit has resulted from the activities of those claiming a renewal of the gifts. For God may honour faith in His power to heal despite misunderstanding of doctrine. But where do these healings in any sense compare with the order of miracles seen in the Scripture record? It would appear that healings among believers who claim miraculous gifts, although more publicised, are in fact no more remarkable than those resulting from prayer by other believers who make no such claims.

It is vital that every aspect of our experience should be governed by the Word of God. In regard to healings, therefore, we should be concerned to ensure that the characteristics of our Master's healing activities are clearly evident. How deeply grieving it is to the Spirit if scriptural principles are violated!

For instance, there are cases where through lack of discernment by a would-be healer the patient's condition is not improved. This is blamed on the patient's lack of faith, an unkind perversion of truth, since the slightest evidence of faith was always rewarded by the Lord Jesus (Mark 9:22-24). It is equally contrary to scriptural principle if healing powers are publicised as a means of propaganda, or used as a means of financial gain.

The Miraculous in Divine Purpose

Generally speaking God has expected His people to walk with Him by faith, not by sight (Habbakuk 2:4; Hebrews 1:1,6; 2 Corinthians 5:7). In line with this principle visible manifestations of miraculous power have been the exception rather than the rule. When it has been granted, the power to work miracles was given only for short periods and for particular reasons. Acceptance that certain miraculous gifts of the Spirit were withdrawn after the special witness of the apostolic period is therefore in harmony with a Bible-wide pattern.

This is confirmed by the Lord's statement in Mark 16:17,18. The Lord said that certain signs would follow them that believe the gospel. Yet multitudes have believed through the centuries without the signs following. If God had intended this statement to be applicable throughout the gospel age, such signs must necessarily have followed continually. Experience proves that this was not implied in the Lord's words. The signs did follow during the apostolic age, but they were not a usual result of belief in the gospel afterwards.

It is important to face facts and see them in clear perspective. Mark 16:17,18 must be interpreted in the light of actual experience. The evidence of history is that the signs have not in fact followed in the vast majority of cases where believers have put saving faith in Christ over the past eighteen centuries. Yet the gospel has so often been proclaimed in the manifest fullness and power of the Holy Spirit.

In view of much misunderstanding about the gifts of the Holy Spirit in our time, readers are asked to consider the subject in the light of the exhortation:

> "Quench not the Spirit; despise not prophesyings; prove all things; hold fast that which is good" (1 Thessalonians 5:20,21)

Did you love *An Introduction to the Holy Spirit*? Then you should read *Back to Basics: A Guide to Essential Bible Teaching* by Hayes Press!

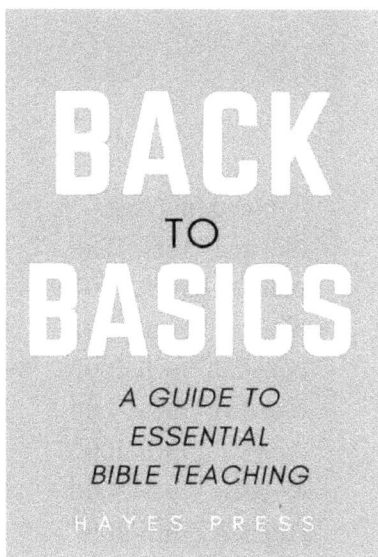

This book uses a combination of teaching and practical content and study questions to explore 8 key topics that are essential to the Christian faith: Knowing God, Salvation, Believer's Baptism, The Breaking of Bread, Understanding The Bible, The Return of Jesus Christ, Spiritual Gifts, Church Life - Why, what, where? This book contains a section of study questions and is ideal for personal or group Bible study.

Also by Hayes Press

Needed Truth
Needed Truth 1888
Needed Truth 2001
Needed Truth 2002
Needed Truth 2003
Needed Truth 2004
Needed Truth 2005
Needed Truth 2006
Needed Truth 2007
Needed Truth 2008
Needed Truth 2009
Needed Truth 2010
Needed Truth 2011
Needed Truth 2012
Needed Truth 2015
Needed Truth 1888-1988: A Centenary Review of Major Themes

Standalone

The Road Through Calvary: 40 Devotional Readings
Lovers of God's House
Different Discipleship: Jesus' Sermon on the Mount
The House of God: Past, Present and Future
The Kingdom of God
Knowing God: His Names and Nature
Churches of God: Their Biblical Constitution and Functions
Four Books About Jesus
Collected Writings On ... Exploring Biblical Fellowship
Collected Writings On ... Exploring Biblical Hope
Collected Writings On ... The Cross of Christ
Builders for God
Collected Writings On ... Exploring Biblical Faithfulness
Collected Writings On ... Exploring Biblical Joy
Possessing the Land: Spiritual Lessons from Joshua
Collected Writings On ... Exploring Biblical Holiness
Collected Writings On ... Exploring Biblical Faith
Collected Writings On ... Exploring Biblical Love
These Three Remain...Exploring Biblical Faith, Hope and Love
The Teaching and Testimony of the Apostles
Pressure Points - Biblical Advice for 20 of Life's Biggest Challenges
More Than a Saviour: Exploring the Person and Work of Jesus
The Psalms: Volumes 1-4 Boxset
The Faith: Outlines of Scripture Doctrine
Key Doctrines of the Christian Gospel
Is There a Purpose to Life?
Bible Covenants 101
The Hidden Christ - Volume 2: Types and Shadows in Offerings and Sacrifices

The Hidden Christ Volume 1: Types and Shadows in the Old Testament
The Hidden Christ - Volume 3: Types and Shadows in Genesis
Heavenly Meanings - The Parables of Jesus
Fisherman to Follower: The Life and Teaching of Simon Peter
Called to Serve: Lessons from the Levites
Needed Truth 2017 Issue 1
The Breaking of the Bread: Its History, Its Observance, Its Meaning
Spiritual Revivals of the Bible
An Introduction to the Book of Hebrews
The Holy Spirit and the Believer
The Psalms: Volume 1 - Thoughts on Key Themes
The Psalms: Volume 2 - Exploring Key Elements
The Psalms: Volume 3 - Surveying Key Sections
The Psalms: Volume 4 - Savouring Choice Selections
Profiles of the Prophets
The Hidden Christ - Volumes 1-4 Box Set
The Hidden Christ - Volume 4: Types and Shadows in Israel's Tabernacle
Baptism - Its Meaning and Teaching
Conflict and Controversy in the Church of God in Corinth
In the Shadow of Calvary: A Bible Study of John 12-17
Moses: God's Deliverer
Sparkling Facets: The Names and Titles of Jesus
A Little Book About Being Christlike
Keys to Church Growth
From Shepherd Boy to Sovereign: The Life of David
Back to Basics: A Guide to Essential Bible Teaching
An Introduction to the Holy Spirit
Israel and the Church in Bible Prophecy

"Growth and Fruit" and Other Writings by John Drain
15 Hot Topics For Today's Christian
Needed Truth Volume 2 1889
Studies on the Return of Christ
Studies on the Resurrection of Christ
Needed Truth Volume 3 1890
The Nations of the Old Testament: Their Relationship with Israel and Bible Prophecy
The Message of the Minor Prophets
Insights from Isaiah
The Bible - Its Inspiration and Authority
Lessons from Ezra and Nehemiah
A Bible Study of God's Names For His People

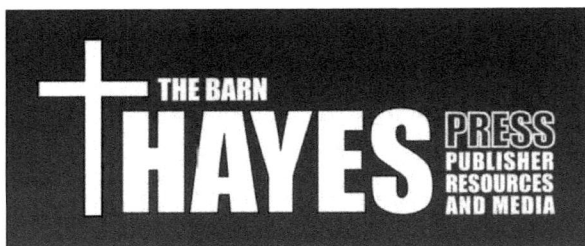

About the Publisher

Hayes Press (www.hayespress.org) is a registered charity in the United Kingdom, whose primary mission is to disseminate the Word of God, mainly through literature. It is one of the largest distributors of gospel tracts and leaflets in the United Kingdom, with over 100 titles and hundreds of thousands despatched annually. In addition to paperbacks and eBooks, Hayes Press also publishes Plus Eagles Wings, a fun and educational Bible magazine for children, and Golden Bells, a popular daily Bible reading calendar in wall or desk formats. Also available are over 100 Bibles in many different versions, shapes and sizes, Bible text posters and much more!

www.ingramcontent.com/pod-product-compliance
Lightning Source LLC
Chambersburg PA
CBHW071829020426
42331CB00007B/1667